AF208063

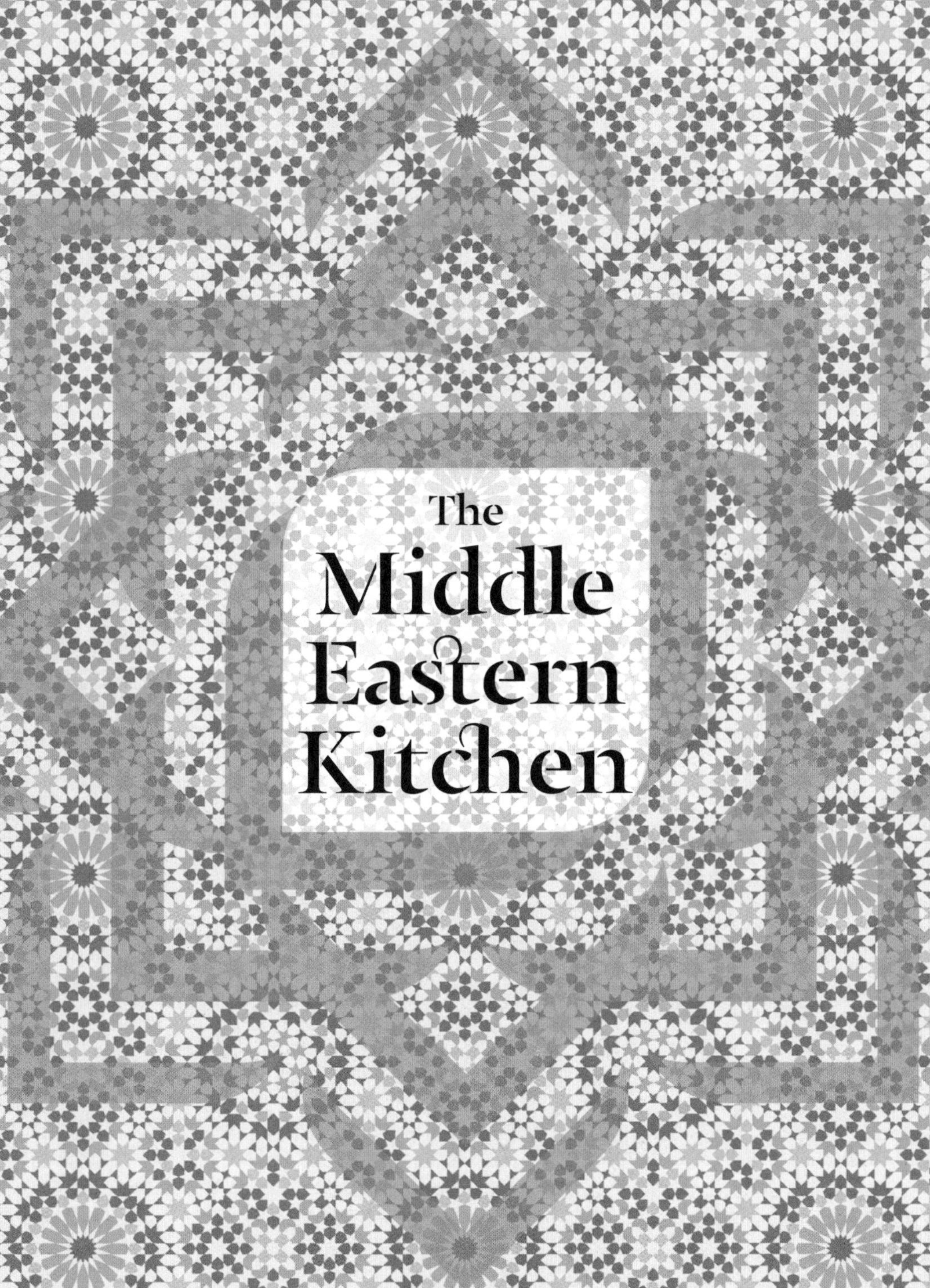

The Middle Eastern Kitchen

The
Middle
Eastern
Kitchen

New recipes by Rukmini Iyer

First published by Parragon Books Ltd in 2016
and distributed by

Parragon Inc.
440 Park Avenue South, 13th Floor
New York, NY 10016
www.parragon.com/lovefood

LOVE FOOD is an imprint of Parragon Books Ltd

ISBN: 978-1-4748-1780-6

Printed in China

New recipes and food styling: Rukmini Iyer
Created and produced by Pene Parker and Becca Spry
Author portrait photograph: Simon Brown
Background images, pattern images, and image on
page 48 supplied courtesy of iStock and Shutterstock

Notes for the reader

This book uses standard kitchen measuring spoons
and cups. All spoon and cup measurements are
level unless otherwise indicated. Unless otherwise stated, milk is assumed to be whole, eggs are
large, individual fruits and vegetables are medium,
pepper is freshly ground black pepper, and all root
vegetables should be peeled prior to using.

Garnishes, decorations, and serving suggestions
are all optional and not necessarily included in
the recipe ingredients or method. The times given
are only an approximate guide. Preparation times
differ according to the techniques used by different
people and the cooking times may also vary from
those given. Optional ingredients, variations, or
serving suggestions have not been included in the
time calculations.

For the best results, use a meat thermometer
when cooking meat. Check the latest government
guidelines for current advice.

Contents

The Middle Eastern Kitchen

From Turkey's yogurt, feta, honey, and pomegranates to North Africa's ras el hanout, dates, and rosewater, the variety of ingredients in the Middle East is equaled only by the diversity of the region's dishes. The food of Iran, formerly Persia, is perhaps the most refined of the area, with its layered spicing and famed jeweled rice dishes. However, Moroccan and Tunisian classics are among the most popular today, including spicy tagines—stews cooked in covered earthenware pots— and fiery harissa. They act as a gateway to the wider region. Iraq, Syria, Lebanon, Jordan, Palestine, Israel, Turkey, and the Yemen all have a wealth of dishes and ingredients reflected in the recipes in this book.

The Middle Eastern cook has an abundance of fresh produce to draw on. There are river and saltwater fish, armfuls of fresh herbs, such as mint and cilantro, sunny Mediterranean vegetables, and a variety of meats, such as lamb and chicken (see page 49), as well as grains, such as bulgur and freekeh. Nuts, such as pistachios and almonds, are used to thicken sauces and add texture, with walnuts popular in Iran and Turkey and pine nuts in Syria and Egypt. Dates, dried apricots, barberries, and raisins bring a sweetness to savory dishes—a popular combination throughout the region.

All these ingredients can be combined and cooked in a dizzying variety of ways. Street food is quickly grilled over charcoal braziers, a home cook may painstakingly roll, stuff, and deep-fry pastries, rich tagines are left to simmer slowly for hours, and crunchy, vibrant vegetables are quickly thrown together in salads.

Spices, from complex blends to a simple sprinkling of sumac before serving, bring depth and flavor to a wide range of dishes. Pickles and preserves (see pages 166–169) add flavor and texture to a meal. Luckily for the home cook, the increasing availability of these exotic ingredients from Middle Eastern grocery stores, gourmet food stores, or the Internet has made Middle Eastern cooking more accessible outside the region.

Most of the dishes in this book are simple enough to throw together for a quick, flavor-packed, weeknight dinner. For weekend cooking, there are plenty of easy, slow-cooked stews and tagines, and the more hands-on kibbeh and small pies are great for an afternoon of adventurous assembly-line cooking.

For special occasions, you can combine dishes from different chapters to create a sharing feast for friends. A particularly good combination is Grilled Eggplant with Pomegranate & Yogurt (page 78), Chicken Kabobs with Za'atar Dip (page 24), Lamb Kofte with Yogurt & Mint Dip (page 66), Fattoush (page 134), and Classic Tabbouleh (page 120), all of which can be prepared in advance. If you're having a lot of people over, a big pot of Persian Jeweled Rice (page 88), Fesenjan Chicken & Walnut Stew (page 40), and Pomegranate Salad with Herbs & Pistachios (page 142) makes the perfect feast to feed a large crowd. Or as an alternative to a Sunday roast, try the Ras el Hanout, Garlic & Thyme Roasted Leg of Lamb (page 82).

Once you're confident with the simple techniques and spice blends in the book, you can modify the recipes to suit your own favorite vegetable or herb combinations. Use cilantro instead of flat-leaf parsley, substitute ras el hanout for za'atar in a spice rub, add more or less chile to a sauce, depending on your preference, and make the dishes your own. In Middle Eastern cooking, as with all recipes, taste as you go along; the perfect combination of lemon juice, sea salt, and freshly ground black pepper, if you like to use them, will vary from cook to cook. Taste, season, then taste again before serving so you can adjust the dishes to suit your palate.

Middle Eastern recipes evolve as you cook them, depending on your taste and the ingredients you have on hand. The region's food and its rich cultural history have similarly evolved into the complex, diverse, and fascinating culinary landscape of today.

Meze

Beet Falafel with Pita Breads

PREP: 1 hour
COOK: 35 minutes
RISE: 55 minutes
SERVES: 4

1 (28-ounce) can chickpeas in water,
   drained and rinsed

1 red onion, finely chopped

2 garlic cloves, thinly sliced

1 teaspoon cumin seeds, crushed

1 teaspoon sumac

1 teaspoon baking powder

2 raw beets, coarsely grated

large pinch of sea salt

large pinch of pepper

3 tablespoons olive oil, for brushing

8 lettuce leaves, shredded, to serve

Whole wheat pita breads

2 cups whole wheat flour,
   plus 2½ teaspoons, for dusting

½ teaspoon sea salt flakes, crushed

1 teaspoon packed dark brown sugar

1 teaspoon active dry yeast

1 teaspoon cumin seeds, crushed

1 tablespoon olive oil

about ⅔–¾ cup warm water

Tzatziki

½ cucumber, halved, seeded,
   and finely chopped

⅔ cup Greek-style plain yogurt

2 tablespoons finely chopped fresh mint

pinch of sea salt

pinch of pepper

Traditionally deep-fried, these ruby-colored falafel are flavored with cumin and sumac, then roasted. Serve in homemade pita breads with tzatziki and lettuce.

1. For the pita breads, mix together the flour, salt, sugar, yeast, and cumin in a bowl. Add the oil, then gradually mix in enough warm water to make a soft dough. Dust a work surface with 1 teaspoon of flour. Knead the dough on the surface for 5 minutes, or until smooth and elastic. Return it to the bowl, cover it with a clean dish towel, and put it in a warm place for 45 minutes, or until doubled in size.

2. When you are almost ready to cook, preheat the oven to 425°F. Dust a work surface with 1 teaspoon of flour. Knead the dough gently, then cut it into four pieces and roll out each piece into an oval about the size of your hand. Let rise for 10 minutes.

3. Lightly dust two baking sheets with the remaining flour, then put them in the oven for 5 minutes. Add the breads to the hot baking sheets and bake for 5–10 minutes, or until puffed up and lightly browned. Wrap them in a clean dish towel to keep them soft.

4. Meanwhile, put the chickpeas in a food processor or blender, in small batches, and process into a coarse paste, scraping down the sides of the goblet several times using a spatula. Pour them into a bowl. Add the red onion, garlic, cumin, sumac, baking powder, and beets, season with the salt and pepper, then mix together, using a fork.

5. Spoon the mixture into 20 mounds on a cutting board, then squeeze them into balls. Brush a large roasting pan with a little oil, then heat it in the oven for 5 minutes. Add the falafels and brush well with more oil. Roast for 20–25 minutes, turning once or twice, until browned and cooked through; break one open and taste to check.

6. Meanwhile, to make the tzatziki, put the cucumber, yogurt, and mint in a bowl, season with the salt and pepper, and mix well.

7. To serve, halve and open the warm pita breads, stuff with the lettuce, tzatziki, and falafel, and serve with any remaining tzatziki.

Cook's tip: *Make a double quantity of pita breads and freeze half the cooked breads in a plastic bag. Defrost at room temperature for 1 hour, then warm in a skillet for 2 minutes on each side.*

This simple, traditional Levantine recipe of crispy meat-stuffed pita breads is a perfect snack. You'll be hard-pressed to get any from the oven to the table—they're too delicious not to be eaten straight from the baking sheet. For a vegetarian alternative, substitute finely chopped cremini mushrooms for the meat.

Arayes

PREP: 25 minutes
COOK: 1 hour
SERVES: 4

3 tablespoons olive oil

1 teaspoon cumin seeds

½ onion, finely chopped

2 garlic cloves, finely chopped

1 teaspoon ground ginger

1 teaspoon ground coriander

1 teaspoon ground cumin

8 ounces fresh ground beef or lamb

2 large tomatoes, finely chopped

3 large pinches of sea salt flakes

large pinch of pepper

¼ cup finely chopped fresh
  flat-leaf parsley

4 whole wheat pita breads

1. Heat 1 tablespoon of the oil in a skillet over low heat. Add the cumin seeds and cook for 1 minute, until aromatic. Add the onion and garlic, increase the heat to medium–high, and sauté for 10 minutes, or until golden.

2. Reduce the heat to low, add the ginger, coriander, and ground cumin, and sauté for 1–2 minutes, stirring constantly. Add the meat, increase the heat to medium–high, and cook for 10 minutes, or until it is well browned, breaking it up using a wooden spoon.

3. Add the tomatoes and a large pinch of salt and pepper, stir, then cover and reduce the heat to low. Cook for 20 minutes, then stir in most of the parsley. Preheat the oven to 350°F.

4. Halve or quarter the pita breads and carefully open the pockets. Stuff each pocket with a heaping tablespoon of the filling, then place on a baking sheet. Brush each pocket on both sides with the remaining 2 tablespoons of oil and sprinkle with a large pinch of salt. Bake for 20 minutes, or until golden and crispy.

5. Serve immediately, sprinkled with the remaining parsley and a large pinch of salt.

Cook's tip: *The meat filling can be cooked up to a day in advance if covered and refrigerated once cool.*

A plate of stuffed grape leaves is one of the most popular meze in the Middle East. The leaves (sometimes called vine leaves) can be stuffed with meat, rice, or vegetables, or a combination of all three. You could easily make a vegetarian version by omitting the meat and doubling the tomato.

Stuffed Grape Leaves

PREP: 45 minutes
COOK: 1½ hours
SERVES: 6

7 ounces drained grape leaves
   (about 28)

½ cup basmati or other long-grain rice

about 3 cups boiling water

2 garlic cloves, finely chopped

1 onion, finely chopped

2 tomatoes, finely chopped

8 ounces fresh ground beef or lamb

2 teaspoons sea salt flakes

1 tablespoon finely chopped
   fresh oregano

1 tablespoon finely chopped
   fresh mint

1 lemon, thinly sliced

1. Separate the grape leaves and put them into a large bowl. Cover with water, then rinse with three changes of water. Cover with more water and soak for 25 minutes, then drain well.

2. Meanwhile, rinse the rice in several changes of water. Put it into a saucepan and cover with 1¼–1¾ inches boiling water. Parboil for 3 minutes, then drain well.

3. Put the rice into a medium bowl. Add the garlic, onion, tomatoes, meat, salt, oregano, and mint, and mix well using your hands.

4. Put a steamer basket in a large saucepan. Line the basket with any torn grape leaves plus the smallest ones. Lay half the lemon slices on the leaves.

5. Lay one of the bigger grape leaves, vein side up, on a work surface. Put a heaping teaspoon of filling in the center. Fold the top of the leaf over the filling, then fold over the two sides before rolling up the leaf into a cylinder, with the folded edge underneath.

6. Put the stuffed grape leaf in the steamer basket. Repeat with the remaining leaves and filling. Your basket should be full, with tightly packed layers. Finish with a layer of lemon slices.

7. Pour 1¾ cups water into the saucepan, cover the steamer with a tightly fitting lid, and bring to a boil. Reduce the heat to low and steam for 1 hour 25 minutes, or until the rice and meat have cooked through and the grape leaves have softened.

8. These are best served hot, but can also be served cold.

Cook's tip: *Vacuum-packed grape leaves, if you can find them, are easier to work with than those from jars.*

These fiery Tunisian-inspired shrimp skewers are great
as part of a meze feast or as an appetizer. Serve them
with a simple salad, such as Classic Tabbouleh (page 120)
or Chickpea, Halloumi, Red Onion & Cilantro Salad
(page 100). You will need four wooden skewers.

Grilled Harissa Shrimp Skewers

PREP: 15 minutes
MARINATE: 30 minutes
COOK: 6 minutes
SERVES: 4

8 ounces (about 24) raw jumbo
  shrimp, peeled and deveined,
  defrosted if frozen

2 teaspoons rose harissa

1 teaspoon fine sea salt

2 garlic cloves, finely chopped

¼ cup finely chopped fresh cilantro

2 tablespoons olive oil

pinch of sea salt flakes

1 lemon, cut into wedges, to serve

1. Mix the shrimp, rose harissa, fine sea salt, garlic, and half
the cilantro together in a large bowl. Cover and marinate in the
refrigerator for 30 minutes.

2. Soak four wooden skewers in water for 20 minutes, then drain
well. Thread the shrimp onto the skewers and brush them lightly
with the oil.

3. Heat a ridged grill pan or heavy skillet over high heat until
smoking hot. Lay the skewers on the pan, reduce the heat slightly,
and cook for 4–6 minutes, or until pink and cooked through,
turning halfway.

4. Serve the skewers immediately, sprinkled with the remaining
cilantro and the sea salt flakes, with lemon wedges for squeezing
over the shrimp.

Cook's tip: *For extra flavor, add the grated zest of an unwaxed
lemon to the marinade. Don't add lemon juice, because it will "cook"
the shrimp before they go on the grill pan.*

Kibbeh

PREP: 40 minutes
SOAK: 30 minutes
CHILL: 1 hour
COOK: 45 minutes
MAKES: 12

¾ cup bulgur wheat

½ onion, coarsely chopped

8 ounces fresh ground lamb

1 teaspoon ground cumin

pinch of pepper

2 teaspoons sea salt flakes

4 cups vegetable oil

Filling

⅓ cup pine nuts

1 tablespoon olive oil

½ onion, finely chopped

1½ teaspoons ground cinnamon

1½ teaspoons ground allspice

1½ teaspoons ground cumin

8 ounces fresh ground lamb

3 tablespoons finely chopped
  fresh cilantro

1 tablespoon Greek-style plain yogurt

pinch of sea salt flakes

pinch of pepper

Cook's tip: If the kibbeh turn brown too quickly when being fried, the oil is too hot and the outside will burn before the inside is cooked. Let the oil cool a little before cooking. Don't leave the pan unattended, don't fill it more than halfway, keep it toward the back of the stove, have the heat no higher than medium, and don't overcrowd the pan or the oil may bubble over.

Take your time when shaping the delicate outer kibbeh shell before stuffing it with spiced lamb or ground beef. It requires patience, but you will be rewarded with meltingly delicious meze.

1. For the shell, rinse the bulgur wheat in several changes of water, then let it soak for 30 minutes. Drain well, squeeze out any excess water, then put into a food processor. Add the onion, meat, cumin, and pepper, then pulse until well mixed. Put into a bowl, cover, then chill in the refrigerator while you make the filling.

2. For the filling, toast the pine nuts in a skillet over low heat for 2–3 minutes. Put into a bowl and set aside.

3. Heat the olive oil in the pan over medium–high heat. Add the onion and sauté for 10 minutes, stirring occasionally. Reduce the heat to medium–low, stir in the cinnamon, allspice, and cumin, and cook for 1–2 minutes, or until aromatic. Add the meat, increase the heat to medium–high, and cook for 10 minutes, or until well browned, breaking it up using a wooden spoon. Mix in the cilantro, toasted pine nuts, yogurt, salt, and pepper. Set aside to cool.

4. For the shell, mix the salt into the bulgur mixture. (To check for seasoning, fry a little of the mixture until cooked.) Divide the mixture into 12 and roll into balls, using wet hands. Press each ball down gently over your thumb to form a deep "cup." Using your thumb and index finger, and your other hand to rotate the cup, flatten out the sides as thinly as possible without breaking the shell.

5. Fill each "cup" with a heaping tablespoon of the filling, then press the top closed, patting the mixture down into the shape of a lemon. Transfer to a plate. Repeat until you've made all the kibbeh, then cover and refrigerate for 1 hour, or until ready to cook.

6. Pour the vegetable oil into a large, deep saucepan until no more than halfway full. Heat over medium heat for 5–10 minutes, or until a cube of bread dropped in sizzles immediately and turns golden within a minute (about 350°F if you are using a thermometer). Working in batches of three to four, fry the kibbeh for 5 minutes, or until golden brown and cooked through. Drain on paper towels and serve hot.

Stuffed roasted vegetables are popular throughout the Middle East. These Turkish-inspired stuffed tomatoes are a perfect vegetarian option.

Stuffed Roasted Tomatoes with Pine Nuts, Feta & Parsley

PREP: 15 minutes
COOK: 30 minutes
SERVES: 4

1 tablespoon olive oil

1 small red onion, finely chopped

1 garlic clove, finely chopped

8 large tomatoes

½ cup crumbled feta cheese

¼ cup pine nuts

⅓ cup finely chopped fresh flat-leaf parsley

pinch of sea salt

pinch of pepper

1. Preheat the oven to 350°F. Heat the oil in a saucepan over medium heat. Add the red onion and garlic and cook for 5–10 minutes, or until translucent. Put into a large bowl and let cool.

2. Meanwhile, using a small, sharp knife, cut a 1-inch diameter circle around the stem of each tomato to form a lid. Using a small spoon, scoop out the seeds and discard.

3. Mix the feta, pine nuts, and parsley into the onion and garlic, and season with the salt and pepper. Stuff the tomatoes with this mixture, pressing it down well using the back of a spoon.

4. Place a "lid" on each tomato and put in a shallow baking dish. Roast for 20 minutes, or until completely softened. Serve warm.

Cook's tip: *Red bell peppers are also good stuffed. Choose small bell peppers and remove the seeds, then soften them in the oven at 350°F for 5–10 minutes before filling and baking them.*

Chicken
Kabobs with
Za'atar Dip
page 24

The meltingly soft marinated chicken contrasts wonderfully with the red onions and red bell peppers in these delicious, spicy kabobs. You will need eight wooden skewers for this recipe.

Chicken Kabobs with Za'atar Dip

PREP: 20 minutes
MARINATE: 1 hour
COOK: 25 minutes
SERVES: 4

1 garlic clove, crushed

grated zest and juice of ½ unwaxed lemon

½ teaspoon ground cumin

½ teaspoon ground ginger

1 teaspoon cayenne pepper

¼ teaspoon ground turmeric

3½ tablespoons plain yogurt

1 teaspoon sea salt flakes, crushed

2 large skinless, boneless chicken breasts (about 5½ ounces each), cut into 1-inch cubes

1 red bell pepper, seeded and cut into 1-inch chunks

1 red onion, cut into 1-inch chunks

1 tablespoon olive oil

Za'atar dip

2 tablespoons olive oil

1 tablespoon za'atar spice

1. Mix the garlic, lemon zest and juice, cumin, ginger, cayenne, turmeric, yogurt, and most of the salt together in a large bowl. Add the chicken and mix until well coated. Cover and marinate in the refrigerator for at least 1 hour, or overnight.

2. Meanwhile, soak eight wooden skewers in water for 20 minutes, then drain well. Preheat the oven to 400°F. Line a roasting pan with aluminum foil.

3. Thread the chicken cubes onto the skewers, alternating with the red bell pepper and red onion chunks, and place them in the prepared roasting pan. If you have leftover onion and bell pepper, put them in the pan, too. Brush the chicken and vegetables with the oil, then roast at the top of the oven for 25 minutes, or until the chicken is cooked through, golden, and slightly charred.

4. For the dip, mix the oil and za'atar together in a small bowl.

5. Let the kabobs rest for 5 minutes. Serve, sprinkled with the remaining salt, with the za'atar dip.

› **Photograph on previous page**

Cook's tip: To grill the kabobs, heat a ridged grill pan over medium–high heat until hot. Lay the skewers in the pan and cook for 15–20 minutes, or until the chicken is cooked through, golden, and slightly charred, turning regularly.

With an irresistible balance of spice, sweetness, and salt, and seared crispy skin, these chicken wings make a very enticing snack. They're perfect as part of a meze meal or for a lazy dinner.

Roasted Chicken Wings with Sumac, Lemon & Garlic

PREP: 25 minutes
COOK: 25 minutes
SERVES: 4

2 tablespoons olive oil

1 tablespoon honey

2 garlic cloves, crushed

1 tablespoon sumac

2 teaspoons sea salt flakes, crushed

grated zest of 1 unwaxed lemon, plus
   1 lemon, cut into wedges, to serve

1 pound chicken wings, cut into
   drumettes and wingettes

¼ cup Greek-style plain yogurt,
   to serve

1. Preheat the oven to 425°F. Mix together the oil, honey, garlic, sumac, salt, and lemon zest in a large roasting pan. Add the chicken and mix until well coated.

2. Roast the chicken at the top of the oven for 25 minutes, or until cooked through and slightly charred with a crispy skin, shaking the pan halfway through cooking to turn the pieces. To check if the chicken is cooked through, push the tip of a sharp knife into a chicken piece; the meat should no longer be pink and the juices should be clear and piping hot.

3. Let the chicken rest for 5 minutes. Serve with the Greek yogurt and lemon wedges for squeezing over the chicken.

› **Photograph on following page**

Cook's tip: A chicken wing is comprised of the tip, drumette, and wingette. The tip is usually discarded, although in Asia it is often regarded as a delicacy. The wingette is the flat middle part and the drumette (which looks like a miniature drumstick) is the upper part. To separate them, wiggle the joint back and forth so you feel where it is connected, then cut through the "hinge" using the heel of the knife, pushing down hard.

Roasted
Chicken Wings
with Sumac,
Lemon & Garlic
page 25

This is a classic Iranian frittata, filled with fresh herbs and walnuts. It makes a wonderful meze dish or light lunch served with salad.

Persian Herb Frittata

PREP: 15 minutes
COOK: 10 minutes
SERVES: 2

6 eggs

2 tablespoons finely chopped fresh dill

⅓ cup finely chopped fresh flat-leaf parsley

⅓ cup finely chopped fresh cilantro

2 tablespoons finely chopped fresh mint

2 garlic cloves, crushed

1 tablespoon all-purpose flour

¼ teaspoon ground turmeric

large pinch of sea salt

large pinch of pepper

1½ tablespoons butter

1 tablespoon olive oil

¼ cup chopped walnuts

1 scallion, thinly sliced, to garnish

1. Preheat the oven to 350°F. Crack the eggs into a large bowl. Add the herbs, garlic, flour, turmeric, salt, and pepper, then whisk well.

2. Heat the butter with the oil in a large, heavy, ovenproof skillet over medium–high heat until foaming. As soon as it stops foaming, pour in the egg mixture, reduce the heat to medium–low, and cook for 5 minutes.

3. Sprinkle the walnuts over the frittata, then transfer the skillet to the oven and bake for 5 minutes, or until cooked through.

4. Using oven mitts, turn the frittata out onto a plate. Sprinkle with the scallion, then cut into wedges and serve.

Cook's tip: *You can make a frittata with most soft herbs, mixed to suit your taste. Basil, tarragon, chervil, and chives all work well.*

Crispy Sumac Squid Rings with Lemon Yogurt Dip

PREP: 25 minutes
CHILL: 1 hour
COOK: 15 minutes
SERVES: 4

8 ounces squid tubes, cleaned and cut into rings

about 1¼ cups milk

1 cup rice bread crumbs

1½ teaspoons sumac

2 pinches of sea salt flakes

1 egg, lightly beaten

3 tablespoons olive oil

1 lemon, cut into wedges, to serve

Lemon yogurt dip
⅔ cup Greek-style plain yogurt
juice of ½ lemon

These squid rings are crispy on the outside and perfectly tender within. Serve them hot as a snack with beverages, or as part of a bigger meze meal.

1. Put the squid in a shallow bowl and pour over just enough of the milk to cover. Cover and chill in the refrigerator for 1 hour to soften.

2. Meanwhile, for the dip, mix the yogurt and lemon juice together in a bowl. Cover and chill in the refrigerator until needed.

3. Put the rice bread crumbs, sumac, and a pinch of salt on a plate and mix well. Put the egg in a shallow bowl.

4. Strain the squid through a colander and discard the milk. Give the colander a good shake to remove any excess liquid.

5. Lay a large sheet of parchment paper on a work surface and line a plate with paper towels. Dip each squid ring in the egg and then the sumac crumbs, then place them on the parchment paper.

6. Heat half the oil in a wok or large skillet over medium–high heat. Working in batches, fry the squid for 3–4 minutes, or until crisp and cooked, turning halfway through, then transfer to the prepared plate. Add more oil to the pan as needed.

7. Serve the squid hot, sprinkled with a pinch of salt, with the yogurt dip and lemon wedges for squeezing over.

Cook's tip: *If rice bread crumbs are not available, use panko bread crumbs instead.*

Falafel Pita Pockets with Tahini Dressing

PREP: 25 minutes
COOK: 12 minutes
SERVES: 4

1 shallot, quartered

2 garlic cloves

1 (15-ounce) can chickpeas in water, drained and rinsed

⅓ cup coarsely chopped fresh flat-leaf parsley

1 teaspoon ground coriander

1 teaspoon ground cumin

½ teaspoon sea salt flakes

pinch of cayenne pepper

2 tablespoons olive oil

2 tablespoons all-purpose flour

½ teaspoon baking powder

2–4 tablespoons canola oil, for frying

Tahini dressing

2 tablespoons tahini

juice of 1 lemon

2–3 tablespoons water

½ teaspoon sea salt flakes

⅛ teaspoon pepper

⅛ teaspoon cayenne pepper

To serve

4 pita breads

1 romaine lettuce heart, shredded

1 large tomato, thinly sliced

½ cucumber, thinly sliced

16 Kalamata olives

4 fresh mint sprigs

This popular Middle Eastern street food is easy to make and usually eaten as a meze appetizer or lunch. Serve hot, fresh from the pan.

1. Preheat the oven to 400°F. Put the shallot and garlic into a food processor and pulse a few times, until chopped. Add the chickpeas, parsley, coriander, cumin, salt, cayenne, olive oil, and flour, then process to a chunky puree. Add the baking powder and pulse once.

2. For the tahini dressing, mix all the ingredients together in a small bowl, adjusting the water content until you have the consistency you like. Wrap the pita breads in aluminum foil and put into the oven.

3. Line a plate with paper towels. Make walnut-size balls out of the chickpea mixture, then flatten them into ¼-inch-thick patties. Heat 2 tablespoons of the canola oil in a large skillet over medium–high heat until hot. Working in batches, cook the patties for 3–4 minutes, or until well browned, turning halfway through, then transfer to the prepared plate. Add more oil to the pan as needed.

4. Slice the pita breads in half. Stuff each half with two to three falafels, lettuce, tomato, and cucumber, and drizzle with the dressing. Serve two halves per person with olives and a mint sprig.

Cook's tip: *This recipe works just as well with whole-wheat pitas. You can try making your own or buy from a local bakery.*

Soups,
Stews &
Tagines

Fava beans are popular in the Middle East, and in this fresh, summery soup the mint brings out all their flavor.

Fava Bean & Mint Soup

PREP: 20 minutes
COOK: 15 minutes
SERVES: 4

2¼ pounds (about 2 cups) fava beans
   in their pods, shelled

2 tablespoons olive oil

1 onion, finely chopped

1¾ cups hot vegetable broth

2 garlic cloves, finely chopped

grated zest and juice of ½ unwaxed lemon

½ cup fresh mint leaves

pinch of sea salt

pinch of pepper

¼ cup Greek-style plain yogurt

1. Put the beans in a heatproof bowl and pour over just enough boiling water to cover them. Drain them well and immediately plunge them into a bowl of cold water. Peel off and discard the outer skins and set the double-shelled beans aside.

2. Meanwhile, heat the oil in a large saucepan over low heat. Add the onion, cover, and cook for 10 minutes, or until translucent, stirring occasionally. Add the beans, reserving a small handful, stir briefly, then pour in 1¼ cups of the broth. Bring to a boil, then simmer for 2 minutes, or until the beans are tender.

3. Stir in the garlic, lemon zest, and half the mint. Process in a food processor, or using a handheld blender, until smooth. Check the consistency and, if you prefer a thinner soup, mix in a little or all of the reserved broth. Stir in the lemon juice, salt, and pepper.

4. Pour the soup into four shallow bowls. Swirl a tablespoon of yogurt into each bowl and sprinkle with the reserved beans. Tear the remaining mint leaves and sprinkle over the top.

Cook's tip: This soup is great served hot. However, it is equally good chilled as a refresher for a hot summer's day. In step four, let it cool to room temperature, then refrigerate.

Kofte, or meatballs cooked in broth, are popular throughout the Middle East. Turkey, Syria, and Iran all have variations on different types of meatballs served in a clear broth or soup with vegetables. Here, they gain extra depth of flavor from the syrupy pomegranate molasses.

Lebanese Seven-Spice Beef Kofte Broth

PREP: 25 minutes
COOK: 20 minutes
SERVES: 4

1 pound fresh ground beef

2 garlic cloves, finely chopped

2 tablespoons finely chopped fresh cilantro

1 tablespoon pomegranate molasses

1 tablespoon honey

1 teaspoon sea salt flakes, plus a pinch

1 tablespoon olive oil

3⅓ cups hot chicken broth

½ savoy cabbage, cored and
    thickly sliced or cut into triangles

pinch of pepper

Lebanese seven-spice mix

1 tablespoon pepper

1 tablespoon ground allspice

1 tablespoon ground cinnamon

1 teaspoon freshly grated nutmeg

1 teaspoon ground coriander

1 teaspoon ground cloves

1 teaspoon ground ginger

1. Preheat the oven to 350°F. For the Lebanese seven-spice mix, put all the spices into a small bowl and mix together.

2. Mix together the meat, garlic, cilantro, pomegranate molasses, honey, 3 tablespoons of seven-spice mix, and 1 teaspoon of salt in a large bowl (store any remaining seven-spice mix in a sealed container for up to one month). Use your hands to work the flavorings into the meat. Divide the mixture into walnut-size pieces and roll them into about 20 small kofte.

3. Heat the oil in a large skillet over medium–high heat until hot. Working in two batches, cook the kofte for 4 minutes, or until golden brown and crisp, turning halfway through, then transfer to a large, lidded casserole dish.

4. Add the hot broth to the casserole dish and bring to a boil. Cover, then bake for 10 minutes. Stir in the cabbage and bake for an additional 5 minutes, or until the kofte are cooked.

5. Taste the broth and season with a pinch of salt and pepper. Serve the kofte and cabbage in deep bowls with the hot broth poured over the top.

Cook's tip: *For a more substantial dish, serve with some fluffy white rice.*

Spicy Chicken Soup with Mint & Couscous

PREP: 20 minutes
COOK: 1¾ hours
SERVES: 4

1 tablespoon olive oil

2 onions, finely chopped

1 red chile, seeded and
  finely chopped

1 teaspoon ground cumin

1 teaspoon paprika

1 teaspoon granulated sugar

2 teaspoon dried mint

1 tablespoon tomato paste

⅔ cup couscous

3 tablespoons finely chopped fresh cilantro,
  to garnish

1 lemon, cut into wedges, to serve

Broth

1 (about 3 pounds) ready-to-cook chicken

1 onion, quartered

1 unwaxed lemon, quartered

10 sprigs fresh parsley, stems only

1 teaspoon coriander seeds

1 cinnamon stick

pinch of sea salt

pinch of pepper

The broth for this classic Middle Eastern soup is made with a whole chicken, which is then torn into strips before being added back to the soup.

1. For the broth, put the chicken, onion, lemon, parsley stems, coriander seeds, and cinnamon stick in a deep saucepan and pour in just enough water to cover. Bring to a boil, then reduce the heat to medium–low, cover, and simmer for 1 hour, or until the chicken is almost falling off the bone. To check it is cooked, pierce the thickest part of the thigh with the tip of a sharp knife. Any juices should be piping hot and clear with no traces of red or pink.

2. Transfer the chicken to a large plate and let cool slightly. Meanwhile, simmer the broth until it has reduced to about 5 cups. Season with the salt and pepper, then strain into a bowl. Remove the skin from the chicken and tear the flesh into strips.

3. Heat the oil in a heavy saucepan over medium heat. Add the onions and chile and sauté for 2–3 minutes, stirring often. Stir in the cumin, paprika, sugar, mint, and tomato paste, then pour in the broth. Bring to a boil, then gradually stir in the couscous. Reduce the heat to medium–low and simmer for 15 minutes. Stir in the cooked chicken strips and simmer for 5 minutes.

4. Serve the soup in shallow bowls, garnished with the cilantro, with lemon wedges for squeezing over the top.

Lamb Tagine with Sticky Dates & Olives

PREP: 20 minutes
MARINATE: 4 hours
COOK: 2½ hours
SERVES: 8

4 pounds boned shoulder of lamb, trimmed of fat and cut into 1½-inch cubes

¼ cup olive oil

2 cups pitted dates

2½ cups pitted black olives

3 cups red wine

10 garlic cloves

⅓ cup finely chopped fresh cilantro

Dry marinade

2 large onions, grated

4 garlic cloves, crushed

1 red chile, seeded and finely chopped

1 teaspoon paprika

2 teaspoons ground cumin

1 teaspoon ground ginger

1 teaspoon pepper

Couscous

4½ cups couscous

grated zest of 1 unwaxed lemon

1 tablespoon fresh thyme leaves

A rich tagine made with tender lamb and sweet dates.

1. Mix all the marinade ingredients together in a casserole dish, then stir in the lamb. Cover and marinate in the refrigerator for 4 hours.

2. Preheat the oven to 300°F. Remove the lamb from the refrigerator. Mix in the oil, dates, olives, wine, and garlic, then cover. Bake for 2½ hours, or until the lamb is meltingly tender, removing the lid for the last 30 minutes of cooking.

3. Put the couscous into a shallow heatproof bowl, pour over just enough boiling water to cover, then let stand for 10 minutes. Mix in the lemon zest and thyme, and fluff up using a fork. Stir most of the cilantro into the tagine and serve, garnished with the remaining cilantro, with the couscous.

This classic Persian feast of chicken cooked in walnut sauce is perfect for feeding a crowd on a special occasion. The chicken is slow-cooked until it almost falls apart, and the wonderful rich sauce gains body and flavor from the combination of ground walnuts and pomegranate molasses. In the north of Iran, this dish, or *khoresh*, is made using duck or game instead of chicken. Serve with Persian Jeweled Rice (page 88).

Fesenjan Chicken & Walnut Stew

PREP: 30 minutes
COOK: 3 hours
SERVES: 8

3⅓ cups walnuts

2 tablespoons olive oil

2 tablespoons butter

2¾ pounds skinless, boneless
  chicken thighs

2 onions, thinly sliced

4 cups hot chicken broth

1¼ cups pomegranate molasses

1 tablespoon packed dark brown sugar

1 pomegranate, seeds only

pinch of sea salt (optional)

pinch of pepper (optional)

¼ cup finely chopped fresh cilantro,
  to garnish

1. Preheat the oven to 350°F. Put the walnuts on a baking sheet in a single layer and roast for 8–10 minutes, or until golden brown, checking them often because they will burn easily. Let them cool completely, then finely grind them in a food processor. Reduce the oven temperature to 300°F.

2. Heat half the oil and half the butter in a large skillet over high heat until hot. Working in batches, cook the chicken thighs for 6–8 minutes, or until golden brown, turning halfway through, then transfer to a plate. (You can use two skillets to speed up this stage, if you want.) Add more butter and oil to the pan as needed.

3. Heat any remaining butter and oil, plus any cooking juices from the plate, in the pan over medium heat until hot. Add the onions and cook, covered, for 10–15 minutes, or until softened and golden brown, stirring occasionally.

4. Put the browned chicken and onions into a large casserole dish. Add the broth and bring to a boil. Reduce the heat to medium–low and, with the broth simmering, add the ground walnuts, pomegranate molasses, and sugar. Stir well, then cover and bake for 2 hours, or until the sauce has darkened from beige to chocolatey brown and the chicken is cooked through and has fallen apart in big chunks.

5. Stir in half the pomegranate seeds and the salt and pepper, if using. Serve in bowls, sprinkled with the remaining pomegranate seeds and the cilantro.

Cook's tip: *For extra richness, use 3½ pounds bone-in chicken thighs, but remove the bones, if you want, before serving.*

Spiced Turkey Stew with Israeli Couscous

PREP: 20 minutes
COOK: 25 minutes
SERVES: 4

1 tablespoon olive oil

1 pound skinless, boneless turkey breast,
   cut into ¾-inch pieces

1 onion, coarsely chopped

2 garlic cloves, finely chopped

1 red bell pepper, seeded and
   coarsely chopped

1 orange bell pepper, seeded and
   coarsely chopped

4 tomatoes, coarsely chopped

1 teaspoon cumin seeds, crushed

1 teaspoon paprika

grated zest and juice of 1 unwaxed lemon

pinch of sea salt

pinch of pepper

2 tablespoons coarsely chopped
   fresh flat-leaf parsley, to garnish

2 tablespoons coarsely chopped
   fresh cilantro, to garnish

1 cup Israeli couscous, to serve

Cumin and paprika combine with fresh herbs to give this Moroccan stew great depth of flavor.

1. Heat the oil in a large skillet over medium heat. Add the turkey, a few pieces at a time, then the onion, and sauté for 5 minutes, or until golden brown, stirring often.

2. Stir in the garlic, red and orange bell peppers, and tomatoes, then the cumin, paprika, lemon juice, salt, and pepper. Cover and simmer for 20 minutes, or until the tomatoes have formed a thick sauce and the turkey is cooked through, stirring occasionally.

3. Meanwhile, fill a saucepan halfway with water and bring to a boil. Add the couscous and cook according to the package directions, or until just tender. Transfer to a strainer and drain well.

4. Spoon the couscous into shallow bowls and top with the stew. Mix the parsley and cilantro with the lemon zest, then sprinkle the herbs over the stew and serve.

Cook's tip: *This is ideal if you are counting calories, because turkey is low fat, especially if you remove the skin.*

This fragrant, golden, lemony chicken stew is the perfect pick-me-up for when you're feeling under the weather. It needs little accompaniment, although a bowl of steaming, buttery basmati or other long-grain rice is delicious with it.

Saffron, Chicken & Vegetable Stew

PREP: 25 minutes
COOK: 45 minutes
SERVES: 4

1 tablespoon olive oil

2 tablespoons butter

½ onion, finely chopped

2 garlic cloves, finely chopped

1 leek, thinly sliced

2 cups finely chopped carrots

pinch of saffron threads

½ cup boiling water

10 ounces skinless, boneless
   chicken thighs, halved

1¼ cups hot chicken broth

4 baby leeks, halved lengthwise

10–12 baby carrots, halved lengthwise

juice of 1 lemon

2 tablespoons finely chopped
   fresh flat-leaf parsley

pinch of sea salt (optional)

pinch of pepper (optional)

1. Heat the oil and butter in a large saucepan over medium heat until the butter stops foaming. Add the onion, garlic, thinly sliced leek, and finely chopped carrots, reduce the heat to medium–low, and cook for 10 minutes, covered, stirring occasionally.

2. Meanwhile, grind the saffron in a mortar and pestle, then add the boiling water, swirl, and pour into a small bowl. Let steep.

3. Add the chicken, saffron water, and broth to the cooked vegetables and bring to a boil. Reduce the heat to low and simmer, covered, for 20 minutes. Add the baby leeks and baby carrots and cook for an additional 10 minutes, or until the chicken is cooked through.

4. Stir in the lemon juice and parsley and season with the salt and pepper, if using, then serve.

Cook's tip: *For extra flavor, use bone-in chicken thighs, removing the bones and shredding the chicken back into the stew in large chunks after cooking. Be aware the chicken takes longer to cook with the bone in.*

This North African take on fish stew has a tomato base and is infused with spices and preserved lemon.

Moroccan Fish Tagine

PREP: 15 minutes
COOK: 1 hour 10 minutes
SERVES: 4

2 tablespoons olive oil

1 large onion, finely chopped

pinch of saffron threads

½ teaspoon ground cinnamon

1 teaspoon ground coriander

½ teaspoon ground cumin

½ teaspoon ground turmeric

¾ cup canned diced tomatoes

1¼ cups hot fish broth

4 small red snappers, scaled, filleted,
  and bones removed

½ cup pitted green olives

½ preserved lemon, rinsed
  and finely chopped

¼ cup coarsely chopped fresh cilantro

2 pinches of sea salt

pinch of pepper

2⅓ cups couscous, to serve

1 tablespoon butter, to serve

1. Heat the oil in a large saucepan over low heat. Add the onion and sauté for 10 minutes, or until softened but not browned, stirring occasionally. Add the saffron, cinnamon, coriander, cumin, and turmeric, and cook for 30 seconds, stirring constantly.

2. Add the tomatoes and broth, stir well, and increase the heat to medium–high. Bring to a boil, then reduce the heat to medium–low, cover, and simmer for 15 minutes. Uncover and simmer for an additional 20–35 minutes, or until thickened.

3. Meanwhile, put the couscous into a shallow, heatproof bowl. Add the butter and a pinch of salt. Pour enough boiling water over the grains to cover by 1 inch, place a folded dish towel over the top, and set aside for 10 minutes, or until the couscous is tender and the liquid has been absorbed.

4. Cut each red snapper fillet in half, then push them into the tomato sauce. Simmer for 5–6 minutes, or until the fish is cooked.

5. Stir the olives, preserved lemon, 3 tablespoons cilantro, and a pinch of salt and pepper into the tagine. Fluff up the couscous using a fork. Serve the tagine, garnished with the remaining cilantro, with the couscous.

Cook's tip: Add a handful of peeled and deveined raw shrimp (defrosted if frozen) to the tagine with the red snapper if you desire, and cook until they are pink. Garnish with a handful of toasted slivered almonds, too, for an authentic Middle Eastern look.

Meat in the Middle Eastern kitchen

Meat is enjoyed throughout the Middle East, slow-cooked with spices in rich tagines, quickly flame-grilled over charcoal as a street-side snack, or ground and blended for meltingly soft kabobs. For feasts or special occasions, a lamb might be spiced and roasted whole, stuffed with rice and raisins. For everyday cooking, inexpensive cuts of meat are used to flavor soups and stews, while ground meat is a popular filling for pies and pastries and more expensive cuts are cooked quickly, often as street food.

Lamb and mutton are eaten all over the region, whether grilled, simmered in stews, or roasted, although in many dishes beef can be substituted for lamb, if you prefer. Ground meat is especially common, because it's a thrifty way to use fatty, cheaper cuts, such as beef or lamb shoulder, flank steak, or lamb neck pieces. If you're making your own ground meat at home, be sure to use this type of cut, because the fat helps to prevent the meat from becoming dry when cooked. In Middle Eastern homes, meat is pounded repeatedly until it is soft and almost pastelike. It creates particulary tender meatballs, kofte (pages 36 and 66), and kibbeh (page 18), which can be eaten by themselves or incorporated in miniature form into soups and stews. You can replicate this pounding process by using a food processor to further grind meat.

When they're not used for ground meat, cheaper cuts such as lamb shoulder and chuck steak are the perfect choice for slow-cooked tagines, biryanis, or stews, because they'll fall apart beautifully after a long, slow cook over low heat. Chicken tagines and stews should also be cooked on very low heat to keep the meat from becoming tough, and again the best cuts are the cheaper thighs and drumsticks, with the bone in for additional flavor.

Organ and variety meats are found in a wide variety of Middle Eastern dishes, with whole sheep heads, stomachs, and feet cooked in broth, known as *pacha* in Iraq, and lamb brain, liver, heart, lungs, testicles, and kidneys used for kabobs in Iran. Lamb or calf brains, often regarded as a delicacy, are eaten crumbed and fried, in salads or as a filling for small pies. In some regions, cooking fat is derived from rendered sheep tail, known as *alya*, although olive oil or clarified butter are now more commonly used.

More expensive cuts of meat should be saved for quick-cooking steaks or skewers. Traditionally, meat skewers are cooked as street food over charcoal braziers, but you can replicate the process at home under a hot broiler or over a barbecue. Thread cubes of tenderloin steak, top loin (strip) steak, lamb loin, or chicken breast onto skewers to make kabobs—the Middle East's most popular street food. You can find recipes for chicken kabobs on page 24 and beef kabobs on page 60.

Iranian Fish Stew

PREP: 30 minutes
COOK: 45 minutes
SERVES: 4

3 ounces tamarind pulp

about 3 cups boiling water

1 dried lime

1 tablespoon olive oil

1 teaspoon fenugreek seeds

1 onion, finely chopped

3 garlic cloves, finely chopped

3 celery stalks, finely chopped

1 tablespoon packed dark brown sugar

2 tablespoons fresh or dried
   fenugreek leaves

1½ cups coarsely chopped fresh cilantro,
   plus 2 tablespoons finely chopped
   to garnish

1 tablespoon all-purpose flour

1½ teaspoons ground turmeric

1¼ pounds firm white fish, such as cod
   or halibut, skinned, bones removed,
   and cut into 2-inch pieces

2 teaspoons sea salt flakes

2 tablespoons clarified butter

8 ounces raw jumbo shrimp, peeled and
   deveined, defrosted if frozen

This herbed fish stew, also known as *ghalieh mahi,* uses a sour-sweet combination of dried lime and tamarind that is popular in Iranian cooking. It is easy to cook and perfect with steamed basmati rice. You can find dried limes, tamarind pulp (or block), and fenugreek leaves in Middle Eastern grocery stores or on the Internet.

1. Put the tamarind into a shallow heatproof bowl, add enough of the boiling water to cover, then let stand for 20 minutes.

2. Meanwhile, grind the dried lime in a mortar and pestle. Heat the oil in a large saucepan over low heat. Add the fenugreek seeds and cook for 2 minutes, or until aromatic. Add the onion and sauté for 5 minutes, or until softened. Add the garlic, celery, and crushed dried lime, cover, and cook for 15 minutes, stirring occasionally.

3. Meanwhile, press the tamarind and its soaking water through a strainer into a liquid measuring cup, using the back of a spoon to push all the pulp through and leaving behind only the seeds and fibers. Scrape underneath the strainer using a clean spoon to get all the pulp. If necessary, top up with enough of the remaining boiling water to make 3 cups.

4. Stir the tamarind water, sugar, fenugreek leaves, and half the cilantro into the onion mixture. Bring to a boil, then reduce the heat to low and simmer, partly covered, for 15 minutes.

5. Meanwhile, mix together the flour and turmeric on a large plate. Dust the fish generously with it, then sprinkle with the salt.

6. Line a plate with paper towels. Heat the clarified butter in a large skillet over high heat. Working in batches, fry the floured fish for 2–3 minutes, or until golden brown, turning halfway through. Transfer to the prepared plate.

7. Add the fried fish, shrimp, and remaining roughly chopped cilantro to the stew. Bring to a boil, then reduce the heat to low and simmer gently for 3 minutes, or until the shrimp turn pink and the fish is cooked. Serve hot, sprinkled with the finely chopped cilantro.

Cook's tip: *You can prepare the base of the stew in advance and store, covered, in the refrigerator for up to a day, then reheat it slowly on the stove and proceed from step five just before serving.*

Tagine takes its name from the earthenware pot in which it is traditionally slow-cooked over an open fire. Freekeh is toasted wheat and makes a delicious accompaniment.

Chicken Tagine with Freekeh

PREP: 30 minutes
COOK: 1 hour
SERVES: 4

1 teaspoon rose harissa

1 tablespoon cumin seeds

½ teaspoon pepper

1 teaspoon sea salt flakes

½ cup olive oil

2¼ pounds mixed root vegetables, such as carrots, turnips, and potatoes, cut into large chunks

8 skinless, boneless chicken thighs (about 5 ounces each)

2 onions, coarsely chopped

2 garlic cloves, thinly sliced

⅔ cup hot chicken broth

1⅓ cups freekeh, rinsed

3 cups water

⅓ cup coarsely chopped fresh cilantro, to garnish

1. Whisk the rose harissa, cumin, pepper, half the salt, and 5 tablespoons of the oil together in a bowl. Put the root vegetables into a shallow dish, pour half the marinade over them, and toss. Put the chicken into another shallow dish and pour the remaining marinade over it.

2. Heat 2 tablespoons of the remaining oil in a large, heavy saucepan over medium–low heat. Add the onions and sauté for 5 minutes, or until softened. Add the garlic and sauté for 2 minutes. Add the marinated vegetables, cover, and cook for 10 minutes.

3. Meanwhile, heat the remaining oil in a skillet over medium–high heat. Add the chicken and cook for 6–8 minutes, until browned all over, turning occasionally. Transfer the chicken to the vegetables. Pour in the broth, cover, and bring to a boil. Stir, then reduce the heat to low and simmer for 30 minutes, or until the chicken is cooked through.

4. Meanwhile, put the freekeh, water, and remaining salt into a saucepan. Bring to a boil, then reduce the heat, cover, and simmer for 25 minutes.

5. Put the chicken and vegetables into a colander set over a large bowl. Pour the drained juices back into the skillet and simmer for 5 minutes, or until thickened.

6. Drain the freekeh and put it into a large serving dish. Arrange the chicken and vegetables on top and pour over the juices. Sprinkle with the cilantro and serve immediately.

Cook's tip: A tablespoon of finely chopped preserved lemons is a good addition with the broth before simmering in step three.

Vegetable Tagine

PREP: 30 minutes
COOK: 40 minutes
SERVES: 4

2 tablespoons olive oil

1 large onion, finely chopped

3 garlic cloves, crushed

1 tablespoon ground coriander

2 teaspoons ground cumin

2 teaspoons ground ginger

1/4 teaspoon crushed red pepper flakes

large pinch of saffron threads

2 red bell peppers, seeded and
   coarsely chopped

2 cups peeled, seeded, and coarsely
   chopped butternut squash or other squash

1 (14½-ounce) can diced tomatoes

2 tablespoons tomato paste

¾ cup coarsely chopped dried apricots,
   figs, or prunes

½ preserved lemon, rinsed and
   thinly sliced

1 bay leaf

14 sprigs of fresh cilantro, leaves and
   stems separated, stems tied together
   and lightly crushed, leaves chopped
   and reserved to garnish

3 pinches of sea salt

2 pinches of pepper

1 (15-ounce) can chickpeas in water,
   drained and rinsed

1 zucchini, halved lengthwise and sliced

2 cups baby spinach

1 tablespoon toasted slivered almonds,
   to garnish

2⅓ cups couscous, to serve

1 tablespoon butter, to serve

Tagines can be made from almost any North African vegetable, but they must be prepared with classic flavorings, such as preserved lemon, dried apricots, ginger, cumin, and coriander, and then slow-cooked.

1. Heat the oil in a large, heavy saucepan over medium–high heat. Add the onion and sauté for 3–4 minutes, or until softened, stirring occasionally. Add the garlic and sauté for 1–2 minutes, or until softened. Stir in the ground coriander, cumin, ginger, crushed red pepper flakes, and saffron and cook for 30 seconds.

2. Add the red bell peppers, squash, tomatoes, tomato paste, dried apricots, preserved lemon, bay leaf, fresh cilantro stems, and enough water to cover by 3 inches. Season with a pinch of salt and pepper. Cover and bring to a boil. Reduce the heat to low and simmer for 20 minutes.

3. Meanwhile, put the couscous into a shallow heatproof bowl. Add the butter and season with a pinch of salt. Pour over enough boiling water to cover by 1 inch, place a folded dish towel over the top, and set aside for 10 minutes, or until the couscous is tender and the liquid has been absorbed.

4. Stir the chickpeas and zucchini into the tagine and simmer for 5–10 minutes, or until the vegetables are tender. Stir in the spinach and let it wilt, then season with a pinch of salt and pepper. Discard the bay leaf and cilantro stems.

5. Fluff up the couscous using a fork. Garnish the tagine with the almonds and cilantro leaves. Serve the tagine with the couscous.

Cook's tip: *Don't be afraid to change the vegetables according to what you like or have available. Eggplants work particularly well, chopped and added with the other vegetables in step two.*

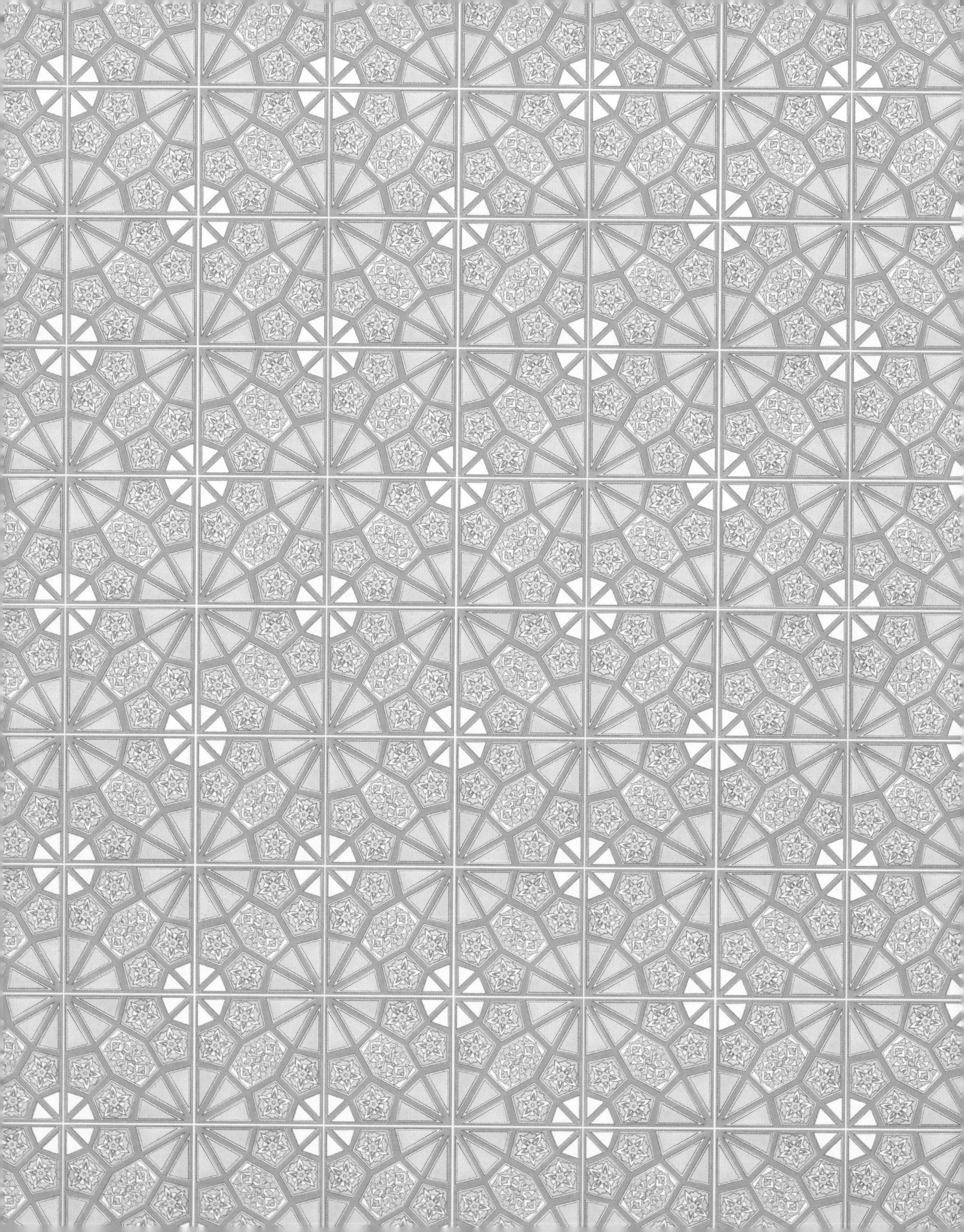

Grills & Roasts

Spicy Grilled Chicken Wraps

PREP: 20 minutes
MARINATE: 2 hours
COOK: 25 minutes
SERVES: 4

2 teaspoons fenugreek seeds

2 teaspoons fennel seeds

2 teaspoons cumin seeds

2 garlic cloves, finely chopped

pinch of freshly grated nutmeg

1 teaspoon cayenne pepper

grated zest and juice of
   1 unwaxed lemon

1 teaspoon sea salt flakes,
   plus large pinch

2 tablespoons Greek-style
   plain yogurt

4 skinless, boneless chicken
   breasts (about 6 ounces each)

2 tablespoons olive oil

large pinch of pepper

To serve
8 whole wheat wraps

¼ cup tahini sauce

2 tablespoons rose harissa

2 tomatoes, coarsely chopped

¼ cup coarsely chopped fresh cilantro

This spiced grilled chicken is traditionally eaten for lunch or a light dinner.

1. Preheat a skillet over low heat until hot. Add the fenugreek, fennel, and cumin and toast for 2–3 minutes, or until aromatic. Let cool slightly, then crush in a mortar and pestle. Put into a bowl, add the garlic, nutmeg, cayenne, lemon zest, 2 tablespoons of the lemon juice, 1 teaspoon of salt, and the yogurt and mix well.

2. Slash the chicken all over using a sharp knife, then put it into a shallow, nonreactive dish. Rub the marinade all over the chicken. Cover and marinate in the refrigerator for 2 hours.

3. To cook the chicken, preheat the broiler to high. Line a baking pan with aluminum foil and place the marinated chicken on the top. Drizzle it with the oil and sprinkle with a pinch of salt and pepper. Broil a couple of inches from the heat source for 20 minutes, or until cooked through, turning halfway through.

4. Let the chicken rest for a few minutes, then tear it into large shreds and serve with the wraps, tahini sauce, rose harissa, tomatoes, and cilantro, for your guests to make their own wraps.

Cook's tip: *To check the chicken is cooked through, pierce the thickest part with the tip of a sharp knife. Any juices that run out should be piping hot and clear with no traces of red or pink.*

Perfect for a barbecue, these spicy marinated beef shish skewers go well with Zhoug (page 162) and a pile of fluffy white rice or flatbreads. Because they're only cooked briefly, under a high heat, it's important to use a quick-cooking steak such as tenderloin. You will need 20 wooden skewers for this recipe.

Beef Shish Kabobs with Mushrooms, Red Onion & Red Pepper

PREP: 25 minutes
MARINATE: 2 hours
COOK: 15 minutes
MAKES: 20

juice of 1 lemon

2 teaspoons ground cumin

2 teaspoons ground coriander

2 teaspoons ground cinnamon

½ teaspoon cayenne pepper

2 garlic cloves, crushed

2 tablespoons olive oil

1¼ pounds tenderloin steak, trimmed of fat and cut into ¾-inch cubes

8 ounces white button or cremini mushrooms, halved or quartered if large

1 large red onion, cut into ¾-inch chunks

1 red bell pepper, seeded and cut into ¾-inch chunks

1 teaspoon sea salt flakes

1 tablespoon fresh cilantro leaves, to garnish

1. Put the lemon juice, cumin, coriander, cinnamon, cayenne, garlic, and oil into a large bowl and stir well. Add the steak, mushrooms, red onion, and red bell pepper and mix well. Cover and marinate in the refrigerator for at least 2 hours, or overnight.

2. When you are ready to cook the kabobs, soak 20 wooden skewers in water for 20 minutes, then drain well. Preheat the oven to 450°F. Line two baking sheets with aluminum foil.

3. Thread the steak onto the skewers, alternating the cubes with the vegetables, and place them on the prepared baking sheets. Sprinkle with the salt. Roast for 10 minutes for medium–rare or 12 minutes for medium, then cut into a steak cube to check it is done to your preference.

4. Let the skewers rest for 5 minutes under foil. Sprinkle with the cilantro and serve.

Cook's tip: If you prefer steak well done, increase the baking time in step three to 14–15 minutes. However, be aware that because the steak is cut so small, it will be a lot tougher than well done steak usually is.

This dish takes minutes to prepare, and makes a delicious, easy midweek meal. The spicy, crunchy topping contrasts wonderfully with the soft fish flakes.

Spiced Baked Cod with Harissa & Pine Nut Crust & Roasted Cherry Tomatoes

PREP: 10 minutes
COOK: 15 minutes
SERVES: 2

¼ cup pine nuts

⅓ cup fresh white bread crumbs or
  ½ cup dried white bread crumbs

grated zest of 1 unwaxed lemon

2 tablespoons coarsely chopped
  fresh cilantro

pinch of sea salt

1 teaspoon olive oil

about 20 cherry tomatoes, still on the vine

2 cod fillets (about 7 ounces each)

2 teaspoons rose harissa

1. Preheat the oven to 400°F. Crush the pine nuts in a mortar and pestle. Put them into a bowl, add the bread crumbs, lemon zest, cilantro, salt, and oil, and mix well.

2. Place the cherry tomatoes on a large baking sheet and add the fish fillets, skin side down, arranging everything in a single layer. Spread a teaspoon of rose harissa over each fish fillet, then top with the bread crumb mixture, pressing down gently.

3. Bake on a high shelf in the oven for 15 minutes, or until the topping is crisp and golden and the fish flakes easily when pressed with a knife. Serve the fish hot with the tomatoes.

Cook's tip: *Substitute the cod with halibut, Alaskan pollock, or any other firm white fish—whatever is freshest and the best value on the day.*

The full flavor of the lemony harissa dressing soaks into the steak, which unusually is marinated after cooking instead of before.

Chargrilled Steak with Harissa

PREP: 20 minutes
COOK: 8 minutes
MARINATE: 10 minutes
SERVES: 2

2 tenderloin or sirloin steaks,
    about ¾-inch thick

pinch of sea salt

pinch of pepper

2 tablespoons olive oil

Harissa dressing

1 heaping tablespoon rose harissa

¼ cup coarsely chopped fresh mint

grated zest and juice of 1 unwaxed lemon

3 tablespoons extra virgin olive oil

pinch of sea salt

1. Season the steaks on both sides with the salt and pepper and rub them well with the olive oil. Set aside for 10 minutes.

2. For the dressing, whisk the rose harissa, mint, lemon zest and juice, extra virgin olive oil, and salt together in a nonreactive bowl large enough to hold both steaks. Add more harissa if you prefer a spicier dressing.

3. Heat a ridged grill pan or heavy skillet over high heat until smoking hot. Put the steaks into the pan, one at a time if they are large, and cook for 1½ minutes on each side for rare, 2 minutes for medium–rare, and 3–4 minutes for well done. If your steak is thinner or thicker than ¾ inch, you will need to adjust the cooking time.

4. Transfer the steaks to the dish containing the dressing and spoon it over them. Cover the dish with aluminum foil and let rest for 10 minutes.

5. Lift the steaks onto plates and slice each one. Pour the juices back into the dressing, whisk, and spoon over the steaks.

Cook's tip: *Sirloin steak is a relatively inexpensive cut; if you buy it from a butcher, ask for a cut from the upper end.*

These herbed, spiced kofte are crisp on the outside and meltingly soft in the middle, with a hidden cube of feta cheese providing a salty kick. You can serve this as a main dish with salads and flatbreads. You will need eight small wooden skewers for this recipe.

Lamb Kofte with Yogurt & Mint Dip

PREP: 30 minutes
CHILL: 1 hour
COOK: 30 minutes
MAKES: 8

1 onion, finely chopped

3 garlic cloves, finely chopped

½ cup finely chopped fresh mint,
   plus extra leaves to garnish

¼ cup finely chopped fresh cilantro
   leaves and stems

1 teaspoon ground cinnamon

1 teaspoon ground cumin

1 teaspoon ground ginger

2 teaspoons sea salt flakes

1 pound fresh ground lamb

3 ounces feta cheese, cut into 8 cubes

2 tablespoons olive oil

1 cup Greek-style plain yogurt,
   to serve

1. Put the onion and garlic onto a cutting board and, using a sharp knife, mince them together into a paste (do not use a food processor or the mixture will get too wet). Transfer to a large bowl. Add just over half of the mint, all the cilantro, cinnamon, cumin, and ginger, and 1½ teaspoons of salt, and stir. Using your hands, mix in the meat.

2. Divide the mixture into eight portions, then roll the first into a ball before flattening it on one palm. Place a cube of feta in the center of the ball, then roll up the sides to enclose the cheese before patting the mixture into a flattened torpedo-shape patty. Repeat with the remaining mixture and feta, then cover and refrigerate the kofte for at least 1 hour, or until firm.

3. Meanwhile, soak eight small wooden skewers in water for 20 minutes, then drain well. Preheat the oven to 350°F.

4. For the dip, mix together the yogurt and remaining mint and salt in a bowl.

5. Heat a ridged grill pan or heavy skillet over high heat until smoking hot. Thread each kofte onto a skewer and brush them with a little oil. Cook for 6–8 minutes, or until crisp and a golden brown crust has formed, turning halfway through. Transfer to a baking sheet and bake for 10 minutes, or until cooked through.

6. Serve the kofte hot, garnished with extra mint leaves, with the yogurt and mint dip.

Cook's tip: *To check the seasoning in the raw kofte mixture, break off a small piece and fry it until cooked, then taste and adjust the seasoning in the rest of the mixture.*

Turkey schnitzel is a popular Israeli dish. Here, spiced up with fragrant za'atar, it makes a satisfying dinner when served with a light salad. Try it in pita breads for lunch.

Za'atar-Spiced Turkey Schnitzel with Tahini Sauce

PREP: 20 minutes
COOK: 8 minutes
SERVES: 2

2 heaping teaspoons za'atar spice,
  plus 2 pinches

¼ cup all-purpose flour

3 pinches of sea salt flakes

½ cup dried bread crumbs

1 egg

1 turkey breast (about 12 ounces),
  or 2 (6-ounce) turkey cutlets

¼ cup olive oil

2 tablespoons tahini sauce, to serve

½ lemon, cut into wedges, to serve

1. Mix 2 heaping teaspoons of za'atar, the flour, and a pinch of salt on a large plate and set aside. Pour the bread crumbs onto a separate plate. Crack the egg into a shallow bowl and whisk briefly.

2. If using a whole turkey breast, butterfly it, then cut through so you have two thin cutlets.

3. Place the turkey cutlets on a cutting board, spaced widely apart. Cover with plastic wrap, then bash each cutlet in turn, using a rolling pin, until it's less than ¼ inch thick all over. It's important to do this properly, because it tenderizes the meat and makes it quick to cook.

4. Dip each turkey scallop first into the seasoned flour, then into the egg, and then into the bread crumbs.

5. Line a plate with paper towels. Heat 1 tablespoon of oil in a large skillet over medium–high heat. Cook the first schnitzel for 2 minutes on each side, adding another tablespoon of oil to the pan halfway through cooking. To check if the turkey is cooked, cut into the schnitzel using a sharp knife. The meat should be cooked through and no longer pink. Transfer the schnitzel to the plate. Repeat with the second schnitzel.

6. Serve the turkey schnitzels hot, each sprinkled with a pinch of salt and za'atar, with the tahini sauce and lemon wedges for squeezing over the top.

Cook's tip: *If you're scaling up the recipe to cook for more than two people, preheat your oven to 125°F. Put each cooked schnitzel on a baking sheet and keep warm in the oven while you cook the remaining ones.*

This is a wonderful way to prepare whole fish. The spices aren't overpowering, but have just the right amount of heat and flavor to complement the fish and give it a crisp crust that contrasts with its soft flesh. The recipe is easily scaled up if you're cooking for more than two people. Serve with steamed vegetables or sea asparagus (also called sea beans).

Whole Spice-Crusted Red Snapper

PREP: 10 minutes
COOK: 20 minutes
SERVES: 2

2 whole red snappers, scaled and gutted

grated zest of 1 unwaxed lemon, plus
  1 lemon, thinly sliced

3½ tablespoons dukkah spice

⅔ cup ground almonds (almond meal)

¼ cup olive oil

¼ cup finely chopped fresh cilantro

2 teaspoons sea salt flakes

1. Preheat the oven to 400°F. Line a large roasting pan with parchment paper and lay the fish on top.

2. Mix together the lemon zest, dukkah spice, ground almonds, oil, cilantro, and salt in a bowl.

3. Spoon 2 tablespoons of the mixture over one side of each fish, pressing it down gently to make a crust. Turn each fish over and spoon 2 tablespoons of the mixture on the other side. Put any remaining mixture in the cavities. Divide the lemon slices between the cavities.

4. Roast for 20 minutes, or until the fish flakes easily when pressed with a knife. Let rest for 2 minutes before serving hot.

Cook's tip: When buying whole fish, look for bright and clear eyes, shiny skin, and bright red gills, and make sure it smells fresh. If the eyes are sunken and dull or it smells "fishy," don't buy it.

This combination of sweet and savory ingredients is popular in the Middle East. Here, the delicately herbed stuffing brings feta and pine nuts together with raisins and lemon. It complements the grilled sardines perfectly. You will need 24 toothpicks for this recipe.

Grilled Sardines Stuffed with Feta, Pine Nuts & Lemon

PREP: 30 minutes
COOK: 6 minutes
SERVES: 4

12 sardines, gutted and heads removed

⅔ cup pine nuts

½ cup raisins

⅔ cup crumbled feta cheese

grated zest of 2 unwaxed lemons,
   plus 1 lemon, cut into wedges,
   to serve (optional)

⅔ cup finely chopped fresh flat-leaf parsley

pinch of sea salt

pinch of pepper

3 tablespoons olive oil

1. Butterfly the sardines and remove the backbones (see Cook's tip, below).

2. Place a skillet over low heat until hot. Add the pine nuts and toast for 5–6 minutes, or until golden, tossing halfway through. Let cool, then grind half the nuts in a mortar and pestle. Transfer them to a bowl, add the raisins, feta, lemon zest, parsley, whole pine nuts, salt, and pepper, and mix well.

3. Spoon 2 teaspoons of the filling into the cavity of each butterflied sardine. Close each sardine like a book and secure, using a couple of toothpicks or a piece of string.

4. Preheat the broiler to high. Line a baking sheet with aluminum foil. Lay the filled sardines on the prepared sheet and drizzle with half the oil. Broil for 6 minutes, turning and drizzling with the remaining oil halfway through. Serve hot, with lemon wedges for squeezing over the fish, if using.

Cook's tip: To butterfly a sardine, open out the gutted fish and lay it, skin side up, on your work surface. Hold the tail with one hand and firmly press along the backbone with the other until the fish is flat. Remove the head if this has not been done already. Turn the fish over and gently pull away the backbone, then cut it out. Remove any remaining small bones using tweezers.

Moroccan-Spiced Roasted Chicken with Stuffed Onions

PREP: 20 minutes
MARINATE: 2 hours
COOK: 1½ hours
SERVES: 6

5 garlic cloves

3 tablespoons Greek-style plain yogurt,
plus 3 tablespoons to serve (optional)

1 teaspoon ground cumin

1 teaspoon ground coriander

2 teaspoons cayenne pepper

½ teaspoon ground turmeric

2 teaspoons sea salt flakes, plus 2 pinches

2 teaspoons ground ginger

1-inch piece of fresh ginger,
peeled and finely grated

1 lemon, halved, plus grated zest
of 1 unwaxed lemon

1 (about 4½ pounds)
ready-to-cook chicken

8 small red onions, peeled

5½ tablespoons butter, softened

1 tablespoon sumac spice

⅓ cup finely chopped fresh mint

pinch of pepper

This roasted chicken is a great centerpiece for a special Sunday meal with friends. Marinating the chicken for a few hours in the spice rub before roasting it improves its flavor and texture.

1. Grate two garlic cloves into a bowl. Add the yogurt, cumin, coriander, cayenne, turmeric, 2 teaspoons of the salt, and the ground and fresh gingers. Squeeze in the juice of half a lemon and mix well.

2. Put the chicken into a large roasting pan, and rub the spice mixture all over the skin and inside the cavity. Put the remaining garlic cloves and lemon half inside the chicken. Cover with plastic wrap and marinate in the refrigerator for 2 hours.

3. When you are ready to cook, preheat the oven to 400°F. Cut a deep cross almost all the way through each onion. Put the butter, lemon zest, sumac, mint, and a pinch of salt in a bowl and mix well. Stuff each onion with the butter mixture, then place them alongside the chicken. Roast for 1½ hours, or until cooked through. To check the chicken is cooked, pierce the thickest part of the thigh with the tip of a sharp knife. Any juices should be piping hot and clear with no traces of red or pink. If the chicken is not cooked, return it to the oven for an additional 10 minutes and check again.

4. Transfer the chicken and onions to a serving platter, cover loosely with aluminum foil, and let rest for 10 minutes. Meanwhile, put the roasting pan over medium heat and skim any excess fat off the liquid. Bring to a boil and reduce by half. Season with a pinch of salt and pepper, then stir in the remaining yogurt, if using. Serve the chicken and onions with the gravy.

Cook's tip: To further check that a whole chicken is cooked, gently pull the leg away from the body. It should "give" and no traces of pinkness or blood should remain.

Grilled
Eggplant with
Pomegranate
& Yogurt
page 78

This dish is perfect for a grazing dinner, and can be easily scaled up if you're cooking for more than four people. You will need a piece of cheesecloth for this recipe.

Grilled Eggplant with Pomegranate & Yogurt

PREP: 45 minutes
COOK: 25 minutes
SERVES: 4 as a side dish, 2 as a main

1¼ cups Greek-style plain yogurt

½ teaspoon sea salt flakes, plus a pinch

1 eggplant, cut into ¼-inch slices

½ teaspoon ground turmeric

2 tablespoons olive oil

3 tablespoons finely chopped fresh cilantro

½ pomegranate, seeds only

1. Line a strainer with cheesecloth and set it over a bowl. Mix the yogurt and a pinch of salt together in a separate bowl, then place it in the prepared strainer. Bring the edges of the cloth up and gently twist them together, then let drain for 30 minutes. Discard the liquid.

2. Sprinkle the cut sides of each eggplant slice with the turmeric and remaining salt and rub it in well.

3. Heat a ridged grill pan or heavy saucepan over medium–high heat until smoking hot. Working in batches, brush one side of the eggplant slices with oil and place them on the grill pan, oil side down, pressing down gently. Cook for 3 minutes, then brush the tops with oil, flip them over, and cook the other side for an additional 3 minutes.

4. Place the eggplant on a large serving platter, in a single layer, if possible. Let cool, then spread each with 2 teaspoons of the drained yogurt. Sprinkle with the cilantro and pomegranate seeds. Serve at room temperature.

› **Photograph on previous page**

Cook's tip: *This dish improves in flavor if kept in the refrigerator for a few hours. Let it reach room temperature before serving.*

This one-dish chicken recipe is rich with the Middle Eastern flavors of harissa and rosewater. It's simple enough for a midweek meal, but special enough for guests.

Roasted Chicken Pieces with Harissa & Rosewater

PREP: 25 minutes
MARINATE: 1 hour
COOK: 1 hour 15 minutes
SERVES: 4

6 bone-in chicken thighs

6 bone-in chicken drumsticks

1 lemon, cut into 8 wedges

⅓ cup slivered almonds, to garnish

3 tablespoons coarsely chopped
   fresh cilantro, to garnish

Marinade

1 tablespoon olive oil

2 tablespoons rose harissa

1 teaspoon rosewater

1 heaping teaspoon Greek-style
   plain yogurt

2 preserved lemons,
   rinsed and finely chopped

pinch of sea salt

1 tablespoon rose petals (optional)

1. For the marinade, mix all the ingredients together in a bowl.

2. Using a sharp knife, make several deep slashes in each chicken piece. Rub the marinade into the chicken and put it into a shallow dish. Cover and marinate in the refrigerator for at least 1 hour, or overnight.

3. When you are ready to cook, preheat the oven to 350°C. Arrange the chicken and lemon in a single layer in a large roasting pan. Roast for 30 minutes, then increase the heat to 400°F and roast for an additional 30–40 minutes, or until deep golden brown and cooked through. Push the tip of a sharp knife into the thickest part of a chicken piece; the meat should no longer be pink and the juices should be clear and piping hot. Cover the chicken with aluminum foil and let rest for 10 minutes.

4. Meanwhile, put the slivered almonds onto a baking sheet in a single layer and roast for 3–4 minutes, or until golden brown, checking them regularly as they will easily burn.

5. Sprinkle the chicken with the cilantro and toasted almonds and serve.

› **Photograph on following page**

Cook's tip: *Rosewater comes in different strengths, so taste your marinade to be sure you are happy with the flavor before using it.*

Roasted
Chicken
Pieces with
Harissa &
Rosewater
page 79

Slow-roasting this spiced leg of lamb will give you meltingly tender meat, and will fill your kitchen with wonderful aromas. This dish creates its own delicious ras el hanout-flavored gravy, but Zhoug (page 162) is also an excellent accompaniment to cut through the richness of the lamb. If you're not cooking for six to eight, consider using a 2¼-pound half leg of lamb, scaling the recipe down by half, and roasting the lamb for a total of 3 hours instead of 3½ in step three—it's too delicious not to serve as a regular weekend meal.

Ras el Hanout, Garlic & Thyme Roasted Leg of Lamb

PREP: 15 minutes
COOK: 3½ hours
REST: 30 minutes
SERVES: 6–8

20 fresh lemon thyme sprigs

8 garlic cloves, peeled, plus 2 heads garlic, halved horizontally

4 teaspoons sea salt flakes, plus a pinch

¼ cup ras el hanout

¼ cup olive oil

1 (4½–5½ pound) leg of lamb

2 onions, cut into quarters

1¼ cups water

pinch of pepper, to serve

1 tablespoon Greek-style plain yogurt, to serve

1. Preheat the oven to 300°F. Strip the leaves from half the lemon thyme and put them into a mortar and pestle. Add the garlic cloves and 3 teaspoons of the salt and crush. Add the ras el hanout and oil, and mix to form a coarse paste.

2. Put the lamb into a roasting pan. Using a sharp knife, make several small slits in the skin. Rub in the spice paste, working it into the slits well. Sprinkle with 1 teaspoon of salt, put the halved heads of garlic and quartered onions alongside it, sprinkle with the remaining lemon thyme, then pour the water around it.

3. Roast for 30 minutes, uncovered. Baste the lamb with the cooking liquid and cover the pan with aluminum foil. Roast for an additional 3 hours, basting every half an hour.

4. Transfer the lamb to a serving platter, add the onions and garlic, and let rest, covered in foil, for 30 minutes.

5. For the gravy, skim the excess oil off the liquid and season with a pinch of salt and pepper. Stir in the yogurt and serve alongside the roast lamb and onions.

Cook's tip: For a more intense gravy, after skimming off the oil in step five, pour the liquid from the roasting pan into a small saucepan and reduce it by half before checking for seasoning and stirring through the yogurt off the heat.

This spiced salmon makes a quick and easy midweek dinner, but tastes spectacular enough for guests, too. Cooking salmon with pomegranate *en papillote* (in a package) gives the fish a wonderful sharpness and sweetness. This goes well with Freekeh, Fava Bean & Pea Salad with Dill & Pomegranate (page 132).

Roasted Salmon with Spices, Pomegranate & Cilantro

PREP: 10 minutes
COOK: 15–20 minutes
SERVES: 4

4 salmon fillets

2 teaspoons ras el hanout

1 teaspoon sea salt flakes

grated zest and juice of 1 unwaxed lemon

2 teaspoons olive oil

½ pomegranate, seeds only

¼ cup coarsely chopped fresh cilantro

1. Preheat the oven to 350°F. Cut out four rectangles of parchment paper, each large enough to comfortably wrap a salmon fillet, and four slightly larger rectangles of aluminum foil. Lay each rectangle of parchment paper over a rectangle of foil. Put a salmon fillet in the center of each parchment paper piece.

2. Sprinkle the fillets with the ras el hanout, salt, lemon zest and juice, and oil, then the pomegranate seeds and cilantro. Bring the long edges of the parchment paper up together, before folding them down a few times to form a crisp pleat over the top of the salmon and tucking the short edges below. Repeat with the foil underneath to form a secure package.

3. Put the packages on a baking sheet. Roast on a high shelf of the oven for 15–20 minutes, or until the fish is cooked through and flakes easily when pressed with a knife. Serve the packages for people to unwrap at the table.

Cook's tip: *Cooking fish in a package is ideal if you are cooking for one, because it is low on mess and high on flavor.*

Rice &
Vegetables

Persian Jeweled Rice

PREP: 20 minutes
SOAK: 1 hour
COOK: 35 minutes
SERVES: 4

2 cups basmati or other long-grain rice

1 tablespoon milk

large pinch of saffron threads

¼ cup clarified butter (see Cook's tip)

1 black cardamom pod

8 cloves

1 cinnamon stick

1 bay leaf

⅔ cup whole blanched almonds

¾ cup unsalted pistachio nuts

1 large onion, thinly sliced

2 large pinches of sea salt

rind of 1 orange, finely pared and cut
  into thin strips

½ cup barberries or dried cranberries

3 cups water

This traditional Persian rice is a festival dish—something to cook for a special occasion or when you've got friends around. It is known as "jeweled" because the almonds represent pearls, the pistachios emeralds, the saffron and orange gold, and the barberries rubies.

1. Rinse the rice in several changes of water, then soak it for 1 hour (if time permits).

2. Meanwhile, warm the milk in a small saucepan. Remove from the heat, add the saffron, and let steep while you prepare the onions and nuts.

3. Heat 3 tablespoons of the clarified butter in a large saucepan over low heat. Add the cardamom, cloves, cinnamon, and bay leaf and sauté for 1 minute, or until aromatic. Add the almonds and pistachio nuts and sauté for 3–4 minutes, or until golden, tossing halfway through.

4. Transfer the spiced nuts to a plate, using a slotted spoon. Increase the heat to medium, then add the onion and a large pinch of salt to the pan and sauté for 10 minutes, or until golden and crisp, stirring occasionally. Add the final tablespoon of butter if the pan looks dry.

5. Drain the rice well, then stir it into the onion mixture. Add most of the orange strips and all the barberries and return the nut mixture to the pan. Cook for 3–4 minutes, stirring constantly.

6. Using the back of a teaspoon, press the saffron into the hot milk to release more color, then pour it into the rice-and-onion mixture. Add a large pinch of salt and the water. Bring to a boil, stir well, then place a tight-fitting lid on the rice and turn the heat down to minimum. Cook for 15 minutes without lifting the lid.

7. Remove the lid, fluff up the rice using a fork, then pour it out onto a couple of large plates to steam dry. Serve hot, garnished with the remaining orange strips.

Cook's tip: To make ¼ cup of clarified butter, melt 6 tablespoons unsalted butter in a small saucepan over medium–low heat until it starts to crackle and foam. Line a strainer with cheesecloth or a clean dish cloth and set it over a bowl. Pour the butter through the lined strainer. The bright yellow melted butter in the bowl is now clarified and can be heated to a high temperature without burning, because the milk solids that usually burn remained in the strainer.

The crisp, crunchy golden base or *tahdig* of Persian rice is delicious. Here, it is complemented by the sunshine yellow color of the saffron rice—hence "double golden." You will need a large saucepan with a tight-fitting lid.

Double Golden Roasted Saffron Rice

PREP: 10 minutes
COOK: 50 minutes
SERVES: 4

1⅔ cups basmati rice

large pinch of saffron threads

2 teaspoons boiling water

3½ tablespoons butter

1 tablespoon extra virgin olive oil

large pinch of sea salt

1. Rinse the rice in several changes of cold water. Put it into a saucepan and cover with five to six times its volume of boiling water. Parboil at a rolling boil for 5 minutes, stirring occasionally, then drain well.

2. Meanwhile, grind the saffron in a mortar and pestle. Add the boiling water, swirl, and pour into a small bowl. Let steep.

3. Put the rice into a large bowl. Mix in the saffron water until the rice is evenly golden.

4. Heat the butter, oil, and salt in a large heavy saucepan over medium heat until the butter stops sizzling. Spread a layer of rice over the bottom of the pan, then pile up the rest of the rice in a cone shape on top—this will help it to steam. Cover the pan with aluminum foil, then a lid, and clamp the foil down well over the sides. Cook for 5 minutes, or until the bottom becomes crispy, then reduce the heat to its lowest setting and cook for 40 minutes.

5. Remove from the heat and let the rice sit, covered, for 5 minutes. Remove the foil and lid and spoon the rice onto plates. Use a spatula to carefully lift the crispy rice from the bottom of the pan, and serve it on top of the rest of the rice.

Cook's tips: When mixing the saffron into the rice, add a little rice to both the mortar and the small bowl the saffron has steeped in to get every last drop of saffron water. To let as little steam as possible escape from the rice, carefully wrap a folded, clean dish towel over the foil and lid around the rim of the pan, but keep it well away from the stove, particularly if using a gas flame.

Lamb Biryani with Dried Apricots

PREP: 45 minutes
COOK: 3 hours
SERVES: 6

⅓ cup clarified butter

3 onions, half thinly sliced
   and half finely chopped

3 pinches of sea salt

1 pound shoulder of lamb, cut into cubes

1 tablespoon olive oil (optional)

1 cinnamon stick

2 bay leaves

8 cloves

3 black cardamom pods

10 green cardamom pods, crushed

2 teaspoons ground ginger

2 teaspoons ground cumin

1 teaspoon ground coriander

½ teaspoon ground turmeric

1¼ cups halved dried apricots

1¾ cups water

large pinch of saffron threads

2 tablespoons milk

2¼ cups basmati or other long-grain rice

about 8½ cups boiling water

⅔ cup Greek-style plain yogurt

Cook's tip: *To rinse basmati rice well, put it in a deep bowl and cover it with plenty of cold water. Swirl the rice, then pour out the water before repeating three or four times. You've washed most of the starch off when the water runs clear as you swirl.*

This luxurious Persian festival dish is perfect for a party. It takes a while to prepare, but you can cook the lamb a day ahead and finish with the rice the next day, if you prefer. It goes well with Greek-style plain yogurt and Pomegranate Salad with Herbs & Pistachios (page 142).

1. Preheat the oven to 300°F. Heat 2 tablespoons of the clarified butter in a large skillet over medium heat. Add the sliced onions and a pinch of salt and sauté for 10 minutes, or until golden and crispy, stirring occasionally. Transfer the onions to a plate, using a slotted spoon. Using the same pan and working in batches, brown the lamb for 2 minutes per side, then transfer to a plate, using a slotted spoon. Add oil between batches, if needed.

2. Meanwhile, heat 2 tablespoons of the clarified butter in a large casserole over low heat. Add the cinnamon, bay, cloves, and black and green cardamom and cook for 1–2 minutes, or until aromatic. Add the finely chopped onions and a pinch of salt, then cover and cook for 10 minutes, or until softened, stirring occasionally. Stir in the ginger, cumin, coriander, and turmeric and cook for 2 minutes. Stir in the lamb and dried apricots, then remove from the heat.

3. Return the skillet to the heat until hot. Pour in ½ cup of the water and let it simmer for a few minutes, scraping up all the flavor using a wooden spoon. Pour this into the spiced lamb. Add the remaining water to the lamb and bring to a boil. Reduce the heat to low, cover with aluminum foil and a lid, then transfer to the oven to bake for 1½ hours. Let cool.

4. Grind the saffron in a mortar and pestle. Warm the milk in a small saucepan. Remove from the heat, add the saffron, and let steep.

5 Rinse the rice in several changes of cold water (see Cook's tip). Add it to a large saucepan and pour in the boiling water. Parboil for 5 minutes, stirring occasionally, then drain well.

6. Stir the yogurt into the cooled lamb. Cover the bottom of a large casserole dish with a few tablespoons of the sauce. Add a layer of the parboiled rice, sprinkle with a few teaspoons of the saffron milk and a pinch of salt, and top with some crispy onions and a layer of lamb. Repeat these layers until you've used all the rice, lamb, and onions, finishing with a layer of rice and saffron milk. Sprinkle with the remaining clarified butter, cover with foil, and put the lid on. Cook on a medium heat for 5 minutes, then transfer to the oven and bake for 40 minutes. Serve.

Iraqi Kitchree

PREP: 25 minutes
COOK: 50 minutes
SERVES: 6

1 cup basmati or other long-grain rice

1 cup red lentils

2 tablespoons vegetable oil

2 teaspoons cumin seeds

2 onions, thinly sliced

3 large pinches of sea salt flakes

1 teaspoon ground turmeric

2 teaspoons ground cumin

2 teaspoons ground coriander

2 teaspoons ground ginger

2½ cups water

1 cup fresh shelled or frozen peas
  (optional)

¼ cup coarsely chopped fresh cilantro

2 large pinches of pepper

To serve

1½ teaspoons olive oil

6 eggs

1¼ cups Greek-style plain yogurt
  (optional)

Kitchree is the original dish behind the popular British "kedgeree." It exists under various names and forms throughout the Middle East and India. It's made of things that households in the region usually have handy: rice, lentils, and onions. While every region has its own variation, this Iraqi version is topped with a fried egg, which complements the soft-cooked rice and lentils perfectly.

1. Rinse the rice and red lentils in several changes of cold water.

2. Heat the vegetable oil in a large skillet over low heat. Add the cumin seeds and cook for 1 minute, or until aromatic. Add the onions, increase the heat to medium–high, and sauté for 10 minutes, or until golden brown and crispy. Transfer half the spiced onions to a plate and season with a large pinch of salt.

3. Add the turmeric, ground cumin, coriander, ginger, and a large pinch of salt to the remaining onions in the skillet and sauté for 2 minutes, stirring often. Add the rice and lentils and cook for 2–3 minutes. Transfer the mixture to a large saucepan.

4. Pour the water into the saucepan and bring to a boil. Stir, reduce the heat to medium–low, cover, and simmer for 30 minutes.

5. Blanch the peas, if using, in boiling water, then stir them and most of the cilantro into the *kitchree*. Season with the remaining salt and a pinch of pepper, adding extra water to loosen the texture, if required.

6. To serve, heat the olive oil in a skillet. Fry the eggs for 3 minutes, or until cooked to your liking (see Cook's tip). Pile the *kitchree* into six shallow bowls, then top with the yogurt, if using, a portion of the reserved fried onions, a fried egg, and the remaining cilantro. Season with a large pinch of pepper.

Cook's tip: *Fry eggs for 3 minutes for a runny yolk. If you prefer a firmer yolk, add another minute or two to the cooking time.*

Mushroom & Eggplant Moussaka

PREP: 40 minutes
COOK: 1½ hours
SERVES: 6

3 large eggplants, thinly
   sliced lengthwise

3 tablespoons olive oil

1 teaspoon sea salt flakes,
   plus 3 pinches

Mushroom sauce

2 tablespoons olive oil

2 onions, finely chopped

2 garlic cloves, finely chopped

1¼ pounds mixed cremini and
   portobello mushrooms, finely chopped

5 fresh sage leaves, finely chopped

5 sprigs fresh thyme, leaves only

2 sprigs fresh oregano, leaves finely
   chopped

½ teaspoon ground cinnamon

1 (28-ounce) can diced tomatoes

½ cup water

3 large pinches of pepper

White sauce

2 cups milk

2 tablespoons butter

⅓ cup all-purpose flour

pinch of freshly grated nutmeg

2 pinches of white pepper

½ cup finely grated pecorino
   or Parmesan cheese

1 egg, lightly beaten

This comforting Turkish dish is a perfect centerpiece to a vegetarian feast, with rich layers of silky eggplants, creamy white sauce, and herbed mushroom sauce. Fresh sage, thyme, and oregano, used to flavor the mushrooms, are all popular in the Middle East. Traditionally, the eggplant slices are fried in hot oil, but this recipe saves time, effort, and calories by roasting them instead.

1. Preheat the oven to 400°F. Line two baking sheets with parchment paper. Lay the eggplant slices on the prepared sheets, brush them on both sides with the oil, and sprinkle with 1 teaspoon of the salt. Roast for 20 minutes, or until softened. Repeat, if necessary, until all the slices are cooked.

2. Meanwhile, for the mushroom sauce, heat the oil in a large skillet over low heat. Add the onions and garlic and sauté for 10 minutes, or until softened, stirring often. Stir in the mushrooms and sauté for 5 minutes. Stir in the sage, thyme, oregano, and cinnamon and cook for 2 minutes. Add the tomatoes, water, and a pinch of salt and pepper. Bring to a boil, then reduce the heat to medium–low and simmer, partly covered, for 20 minutes.

3. For the white sauce, heat the milk in a milk pan until just below boiling point. Meanwhile, heat the butter in a saucepan over medium–low heat until it starts to foam. Add the flour to the butter and stir constantly for 2 minutes, until you have a smooth mixture that comes away cleanly from the sides of the pan. Pour in the hot milk, a little at a time, stirring well between each addition to prevent lumps from forming, until you have a thick, smooth sauce.

4. Increase the heat to medium–high and bring the white sauce to a boil, stirring constantly. Cook for 3 minutes, then stir in the nutmeg and white pepper. Remove from the heat and stir in the cheese and a pinch of salt and black pepper. Let cool, then whisk in the egg.

5. To assemble the moussaka, put a layer of eggplant in the bottom of a lasagne dish, spread one-third of the mushroom sauce on top, then add another layer of eggplant and an additional third of the mushroom sauce. Repeat with a final layer of both. Spread the white sauce evenly over the top, then season with the remaining salt and black pepper.

6. Bake for 30–35 minutes, or until golden and puffed up. Let cool for 10–15 minutes before serving.

Spices in the Middle Eastern Kitchen

The best way to understand the variety of spices available to the Middle Eastern cook is to visit one of the region's souks or bazaars. Imagine yourself in the souk, surrounded by baskets of piled spices. Many will be known to you—star anise, allspice berries, cinnamon sticks, cardamom pods, cloves, nutmeg, dried chiles and peppercorns, or caraway, coriander, cumin, fennel, and fenugreek seeds— all piled up in glorious, headily aromatic abundance. It's a far cry from the tiny, uniform glass jars you find in the spice aisle of your local supermarket. When you buy these spices at home, it's always best to choose the whole spice, as you would at the souk, and grind them in small quantities as needed; that way, they'll stay fresh and aromatic. Save time by using an electric coffee grinder for this, although a mortar and pestle is, of course, the traditional method.

More unusual spices at the souk include baskets of whole turmeric, which looks like fresh ginger, but smaller and bright yellow, as well as piles of fenugreek leaves, sumac, cassia bark, and dried chamomile. Prettiest of all are the piles of pink, jewel-like rosebuds, which are used in pilafs, chicken dishes, and sweet treats. Behind the counter, you'll find highly prized and expensive Iranian saffron, used throughout the region for special occasions and festival cooking. Make saffron go a little further at home by pounding a small pinch with sea salt flakes in a mortar and pestle and storing the delicately colored salt in a salt shaker to finish off dishes with a burst of saffron flavor.

You'll also find many speciality regional ingredients at the spice souk, including piles of musty gray-green dried limes, piled in mounds like hollow, misshapen golf balls. In hot countries, you can dry your own limes in the sun. Both dried limes and tamarind are used to give a distinctive and delicious sour flavor to Iranian and Iraqi cooking. In Moroccan cooking, preserved lemons are used for a similar purpose; try the recipe on page 166, because they're easy to make.

All the spice shops in the souk sell similar whole spices, but what really sets them apart are the house blends offered. The best blend will be ras el hanout—anything between 12 and 100 of the finest spices in the shop, made to a closely guarded secret recipe. Other popular blends, which you can find in Middle Eastern grocery stores or on the Internet, include za'atar (dried thyme, salt, and toasted sesame seeds) and dukkah (pounded cumin seeds, hazelnuts, sesame seeds, and coriander seeds), both of which are popular mixed with olive oil as a dip for pita breads. More speciality blends include Egyptian *quatre-épice* (pepper, nutmeg, cloves, and cinnamon), Lebanese seven-spice mix (nutmeg, ginger, allspice, coriander, cloves, cinnamon, and black pepper), or the pungent *baharat* (which may include coriander seeds, black pepper, cloves, cardamom, cumin seeds, cinnamon, sweet paprika, nutmeg, sumac, saffron, turmeric, and chiles).

This summery salad tastes best served immediately, with the halloumi still hot from the pan. It can also be prepared a few hours in advance and stored in the refrigerator, then brought back to room temperature before serving. It's best eaten the day it's made, because the halloumi tends to lose its flavor if it sits in a salad for too long.

Chickpea, Halloumi, Red Onion & Cilantro Salad

PREP: 10 minutes
COOK: 12 minutes
SERVES: 4

8 ounces halloumi, sliced

1 (15-ounce) can chickpeas in water, drained and rinsed

1 red onion, finely chopped

3 tablespoons finely chopped fresh cilantro

juice of 1½ lemons

1 tablespoon extra virgin olive oil

pinch of sea salt (optional)

pinch of pepper (optional)

1. Heat a ridged grill pan or heavy skillet over high heat until smoking hot. Working in batches, cook the halloumi in the dry pan for 4–6 minutes, or until charred, golden, and crispy in places, turning halfway through. Transfer to a cutting board and let cool slightly, then cut into ½-inch cubes.

2. Mix together the halloumi, chickpeas, red onion, cilantro, lemon juice, and oil in a large salad bowl. Mix in the salt and pepper, if using, then serve immediately.

Cook's tips: *Try this salad with Classic Tabbouleh (page 120). If you are struggling to find halloumi, you can try queso para freir from a nearby Mexican grocery store.*

This North African breakfast of eggs baked in fiery spiced bell peppers, tomatoes, onions, and garlic is popular throughout the Middle East. Serve it as a breakfast, or with a pile of flatbreads as a light dinner.

Shakshouka

PREP: 20 minutes
COOK: 45 minutes
SERVES: 4

3 tablespoons olive oil

1 teaspoon cumin seeds

2 red onions, thinly sliced

2 garlic cloves, finely chopped

1 red chile, seeded and
    finely chopped

1 teaspoon sea salt flakes, plus a pinch

2 red bell peppers, seeded and thinly sliced

3 tomatoes, coarsely chopped

2 pinches of pepper

4 eggs

2 teaspoons za'atar spice

1. Preheat the oven to 350°F. Heat the oil in a large ovenproof skillet over low heat. Add the cumin and cook for 1–2 minutes, or until aromatic. Add the red onions, garlic, chile, and 1 teaspoon of salt and sauté for 5 minutes, or until softened, stirring often.

2. Add the red bell peppers and increase the heat to medium. Sauté for 1 minute, stirring constantly. Reduce the heat to low, cover, and cook for an additional 20 minutes, stirring occasionally.

3. Add the tomatoes and a pinch of salt and pepper and cook for 5 minutes.

4. Using a wooden spoon, make four deep egg-size indentations in the sauce, then crack an egg into each one. Sprinkle the za'atar over the eggs and sauce.

5. Bake for 10 minutes, or until just set. Sprinkle with the remaining pinch of pepper and serve hot.

Cook's tip: Keep an eye on the Shakshouka as it cooks and take it out of the oven when the eggs are done to your preference—for well-done eggs, it may need to be baked for up to 15 minutes.

Capture the flavors and colors of Morocco with this spicy brown rice salad flecked with jewel-like dried apricots and glistening raisins and tossed with health-boosting kale.

Moroccan Chicken with Rice

PREP: 15 minutes
COOK: 35 minutes
SERVES: 4

1½ cups quick-cooking brown rice

2 teaspoons tomato paste

1 pound skinless, boneless chicken breasts

½ cup coarsely chopped dried apricots

⅓ cup raisins

½ preserved lemon, rinsed and
    finely chopped

1 small red onion, finely chopped

3 tablespoons pine nuts

1¼ cups shredded kale

Dressing
2 teaspoons rose harissa

¼ cup olive oil

juice of 1 lemon

pinch of sea salt

pinch of pepper

1. Put the rice into a saucepan and cover with boiling water. Bring back to a boil, then simmer for 25—30 minutes, or until just tender. Drain, then transfer to a salad bowl.

2. Meanwhile, for the dressing, put the harissa, oil, and lemon juice in a screw-top jar and season with the salt and pepper. Screw on the lid and shake well.

3. Spoon 2 tablespoons of the dressing into a bowl and mix in the tomato paste. Preheat the broiler to high and line the grill pan with aluminum foil. Put the chicken on the foil in a single layer. Brush some of the tomato dressing over it, then broil for 15—18 minutes, or until golden and cooked through, turning and brushing with the remaining tomato dressing halfway through. Cut through the middle of a breast to check that the meat is no longer pink. Any juices that run out should be clear and piping hot with steam rising. Cover and let cool.

4. Drizzle the remaining dressing over the rice. Add the dried apricots, raisins, preserved lemon, and red onion, then toss and let cool. Toast the pine nuts in a skillet over medium heat for 2—3 minutes. Blanch the kale for 2—3 minutes. Add the pine nuts and kale to the salad and stir. Thinly slice the chicken, arrange it over the salad, and serve.

Cook's tip: *Try to find unsulfured (dark) dried apricots instead of the sulfured (bright orange) ones, because they are more natural and fruity tasting.*

Spiced Vegetable & Halloumi Skewers

PREP: 25 minutes
COOK: 30 minutes
SERVES: 8

8 ounces cremini mushrooms, halved
    or quartered, depending on size

9 ounces halloumi or queso para freir,
    cut into 5/8-inch cubes

1 large eggplant, cut into 3/4-inch chunks

3 cups (about 1 pound) cherry tomatoes

1 tablespoon ras el hanout

1 teaspoon sea salt flakes,
    plus a large pinch

3 tablespoons olive oil

These spiced skewers make a great vegetarian option for barbecues and are perfect for a crowd. Consider serving them with a pile of flatbreads (page 174), Greek-style plain yogurt, Tahini Sauce (page 165), and Rose Harissa (page 154) for people to create their own wraps. You will need 16 wooden skewers for this recipe.

1. Preheat the oven to 350°F. Soak 16 wooden skewers in water for 20 minutes, then drain well.

2. Put the mushrooms, halloumi, eggplant, and cherry tomatoes in a large bowl and toss well. Add the ras el hanout, 1 teaspoon of salt, and the oil and toss again.

3. Thread the vegetables and halloumi onto the skewers in any combination, then place them on two large baking sheets. Roast for 30 minutes, or until the vegetables are tender. Sprinkle with a large pinch of salt and serve two skewers per person.

Cook's tip: If you prefer, assemble the skewers in advance, and let them marinate for a few hours in the refrigerator before cooking.

Warm Red Lentils with Spinach

PREP: 25 minutes
COOK: 30 minutes
SERVES: 4

2 tablespoons olive oil

2 teaspoons cumin seeds

2 garlic cloves, crushed

¾-inch piece of fresh ginger,
  peeled and finely grated

1½ cups red lentils

3 cups hot vegetable broth

2 tablespoons coarsely chopped
  fresh mint

2 tablespoons coarsely chopped
  fresh cilantro

2 red onions, thinly sliced

1 (6-ounce) package baby spinach

1 teaspoon hazelnut oil

5½ ounces soft goat cheese

¼ cup Greek-style plain yogurt

pinch of pepper

This spiced, earthy salad is freshened up by the addition of mint and cilantro leaves. It goes particularly well with Pomegranate Salad with Herbs & Pistachios (page 142).

1. Heat 1 tablespoon of the olive oil in a large saucepan over medium heat. Add the cumin, garlic, and ginger and stir-fry for 2 minutes. Stir in the lentils, then add the broth, a ladleful at a time, simmering and stirring occasionally until each ladleful has been absorbed before adding the next one; this will take about 20 minutes in total. Remove from the heat, then stir in the mint and cilantro.

2. Meanwhile, heat the remaining olive oil in a skillet over medium–low heat. Add the red onions and cook for 10 minutes, or until softened and lightly browned, stirring often.

3. Put the baby spinach and hazelnut oil in a bowl and toss gently. Divide among four shallow bowls.

4. Put the goat cheese and yogurt into a small bowl, season with pepper, then mash.

5. Spoon the lentils onto the spinach, top with the onions, then spoon on the goat cheese and yogurt and serve.

Cook's tip: *It's important not to overcook lentils for a salad, because they should have some bite.*

Okra is popular throughout the Middle East, and is served here in a Sephardi-inspired rich garlic, tomato, and chickpea sauce. Roasting the okra separately helps prevent it from becoming sticky.

Okra with Chickpeas, Tomatoes & Garlic

PREP: 25 minutes
COOK: 45 minutes
SERVES: 6

1¼ pounds okra

2 teaspoons sumac spice

grated zest and juice of
  1 unwaxed lemon

3 pinches of sea salt

2 pinches of pepper

¼ cup olive oil

1 teaspoon coriander seeds

1 large onion, thinly sliced

4 tomatoes, coarsely chopped

2 garlic cloves, crushed

1 (15-ounce) can chickpeas in water,
  drained and rinsed

⅔ cup coarsely chopped fresh cilantro,
  plus 1 tablespoon to garnish

½ cup water

1. Preheat the oven to 400°F. Mix the okra, sumac, lemon zest, a pinch of salt and pepper, and half the oil together in a roasting pan. Roast for 20 minutes, or until tender.

2. Meanwhile, heat the remaining oil in a skillet over low heat. Add the coriander and cook for 2 minutes, or until aromatic. Increase the heat to medium–high, add the onion and a pinch of salt, and sauté for 10 minutes, or until golden brown, stirring occasionally.

3. Add the tomatoes and garlic to the onion and simmer for 5 minutes, breaking up any larger pieces of tomato using a wooden spoon. Add the chickpeas, cilantro, and water, bring to a boil, then reduce the heat to a simmer, cover with a lid, and cook for 15 minutes. Remove the lid and cook for an additional 5 minutes, or until thickened.

4. Stir in the roasted okra, then season with the lemon juice and a pinch of salt and pepper. Garnish with the remaining chopped cilantro and serve.

Cook's tip: *If you rinse okra before roasting it, be sure to dry it thoroughly with paper towels or it will steam instead of roast.*

These mildly spiced roasted veggies make a great light meal served with couscous or rice, and they are just as good served as a side dish for roasted chicken or fish.

Cumin-Roasted Beet & Carrots with Tahini Dressing

PREP: 15 minutes
COOK: 1 hour
SERVES: 2

8 small raw beets, quartered

8 carrots, cut into wedges the same size as the beet quarters

1 teaspoon cumin seeds

1 teaspoon coriander seeds

1 teaspoon sea salt flakes

2 tablespoons olive oil

2½ tablespoons pistachio nuts, toasted and coarsely chopped (see Cook's tip), to garnish

Tahini dressing

1 teaspoon tahini

1 tablespoon Greek-style plain yogurt

1 tablespoon extra virgin olive oil

juice of ½ lemon

pinch of sea salt

1. Preheat the oven to 350°F. Mix together the beets, carrots, cumin, coriander, salt, and olive oil in a roasting pan. Roast for 1 hour, or until tender.

2. Meanwhile, for the dressing, whisk together the tahini, yogurt, extra virgin olive oil, and lemon juice in a bowl, then season with the salt.

3. Transfer the vegetables to a serving platter. Dot the dressing over them, sprinkle with the pistachio nuts, and serve immediately.

Cook's tip: To toast a large quantity of whole nuts, preheat your oven to 350°F, spread the nuts onto a baking sheet in a single layer, then roast for 5–10 minutes. Check them regularly, because they burn easily. For smaller quantities of nuts, place them in a dry skillet large enough to hold them in a single layer, and toast them over low heat for 5–6 minutes, or until they are evenly golden and smell toasty, shaking the pan every couple of minutes. Do not leave them unattended—they will burn as soon as you turn your back.

This dish is filling enough to eat as a vegetarian main dish, but makes a great side dish for lamb or chicken, too.

Spiced Roasted Cauliflower with Almonds & Tahini Dressing

PREP: 10 minutes
COOK: 35 minutes
SERVES: 4

1 large cauliflower, cut into small florets

1 teaspoon baharat spice mix

1 teaspoon sea salt flakes

2 tablespoons olive oil

3 tablespoons blanched almonds, toasted, to garnish

3 tablespoons coarsely chopped fresh cilantro, to garnish

Tahini dressing

4 teaspoons tahini

¼ cup Greek-style plain yogurt

juice of ½ lemon

pinch of sea salt

pinch of pepper

1. Preheat the oven to 400°F. Put the cauliflower into a large roasting pan. Sprinkle with the baharat spice mix, salt, and oil and mix well. Roast for 25–35 minutes, or until lightly charred but still with some bite.

2. Meanwhile, for the dressing, mix the tahini, yogurt, and lemon juice together in a bowl, then season with the salt and pepper.

3. Transfer the cauliflower to a serving plate, dot with the tahini dressing, and sprinkle with the almonds and cilantro. Serve immediately.

Cook's tip: If you can't find baharat spice mix, use an equal mixture of ground coriander, ground cumin, and ground cinnamon instead.

Lebanese Seven-Spice Roasted Squash with Feta & Pine Nuts

PREP: 15 minutes
COOK: 45 minutes
SERVES: 6

1 (about 2¼ pound) butternut squash or other squash, halved and cut into wedges

2 teaspoons sea salt flakes, plus a pinch

2 tablespoons extra virgin olive oil

pinch of pepper

¼ cup pine nuts

½ cup crumbled feta cheese

3 scallions, thinly sliced

1 cup arugula

Lebanese seven-spice mix

1 tablespoon pepper

1 tablespoon ground allspice

1 tablespoon ground cinnamon

1 teaspoon freshly grated nutmeg

1 teaspoon ground coriander

1 teaspoon ground cloves

1 teaspoon ground ginger

This is great for a crowd, and you can use whatever type of winter squash is in season. The crunchy scallions and salty feta provide a great contrast to the smoky spiced squash.

1. Preheat the oven to 400°F. For the Lebanese seven-spice mix, put all the spices in small bowl and mix together.

2. Put the squash in a roasting pan and sprinkle with 2 tablespoons of seven-spice mix and 2 teaspoons of salt, then drizzle with the oil and toss well, using your hands. Roast for 45 minutes, or until tender. Let cool slightly, then season with a pinch of salt and pepper.

3. Toast the pine nuts in a skillet over medium heat for 2–3 minutes. Sprinkle them and the feta, scallions, and arugula over the squash, then serve immediately.

Cook's tip: *Rinse and dry the squash seeds, then sprinkle them into a skillet with a teaspoon of seven-spice mix and dry-fry until golden. Sprinkle with sea salt. Use these instead of the pine nuts to top the dish, or eat as a snack. Keep any unused seven-spice mix in an airtight jar.*

There are numerous variations of batata harra, a spiced Lebanese potato dish. Although some include bell peppers and onions, this recipe is all about the enticing crispy potatoes, because they tend to lose their crunch once other vegetables are introduced. To finish the dish, herbs are fried in hot butter to bring out their flavor—a classic Middle Eastern technique.

Batata Harra

PREP: 10 minutes
COOK: 50 minutes
MARINATE: 1 hour
SERVES: 4

9 floury potatoes, such as russets,
    cut into ⅝-inch chunks

3 garlic cloves, crushed

½ teaspoon cayenne pepper

2 tablespoons olive oil

1 teaspoon sea salt flakes, plus a pinch

1½ tablespoons butter

3 tablespoons finely chopped fresh cilantro

juice of ½ lemon

pinch of pepper

1. Mix together the potatoes, garlic, cayenne, and 1 tablespoon of the oil in a large bowl. Cover and marinate in the refrigerator for at least 1 hour, or up to 4 hours.

2. When you are ready to cook, preheat the oven to 400°F. Put the potatoes into a large roasting pan and, if damp, dry them with paper towels. Mix with another tablespoon of oil and a teaspoon of salt, then roast on a high shelf for 40–50 minutes, or until golden brown and crisp.

3. When the potatoes are cooked, heat the butter in a large skillet over low heat until it stops foaming. Stir in the cilantro and cook for 1 minute. Add the roasted potatoes, then the lemon juice and toss. Season with a pinch of salt and pepper, then serve immediately.

Cook's tip: *Herbs are often interchangeable in Middle Eastern recipes. In this dish, cilantro is a good match, but you can use fresh flat-leaf parsley, if you prefer.*

Salads, Grains & Couscous

Tabbouleh is a summery, fresh, and aromatic green salad, in which soft herbs take center stage and onion adds piquancy. It is served with many different dishes in the Middle East.

Classic Tabbouleh

PREP: 20 minutes
COOK: 10 minutes
SERVES: 6

¼ cup bulgur wheat, rinsed

1⅔ cups finely chopped fresh
   flat-leaf parsley

½ cup finely chopped fresh mint

½ onion, minced

2 tomatoes, finely chopped

juice of ½ lemon

2 tablespoons extra virgin olive oil

pinch of sea salt

pinch of pepper

1. Put the bulgur wheat into a saucepan and cover with four to five times its volume of boiling water. Bring to a boil, then reduce the heat and simmer, uncovered, for 8–10 minutes, or until cooked but with some bite. Drain, then rinse and put into a large, shallow salad bowl. Let cool to room temperature.

2. Mix the parsley, mint, onion, tomatoes, lemon juice, and oil into the bulgur wheat and season with the salt and pepper.

Cook's tip: *Customize your tabbouleh by adding finely chopped fresh cilantro, lovage, or celery leaves.*

Chicken with Pomegranate & Beet Tabbouleh

PREP: 20 minutes
COOK: 30 minutes
SERVES: 4

1¼ cups wheat berries

4 raw beets (about 12 ounces),
  cut into cubes

1 pound skinless, boneless
  chicken breasts, thinly sliced

1 small red onion, thinly sliced

12 cherry tomatoes, halved

1 small pomegranate, seeds only

2 tablespoons coarsely chopped fresh mint

2½ cups baby spinach

Dressing
juice of 1 lemon

¼ cup extra virgin olive oil

2 garlic cloves, finely chopped

1 teaspoon packed light brown sugar

pinch of salt

pinch of pepper

This version of tabbouleh combines whole-grain wheat berries with traditional pomegranate for a modern twist on the classic Middle Eastern dish.

1. Fill the bottom of a steamer halfway with water, bring to a boil, then add the wheat berries to the water. Put the beets into the steamer top, cover with a lid, and steam for 20–25 minutes, or until the wheat berries and beets are tender. Drain the wheat berries.

2. Meanwhile, for the dressing, put the lemon juice, oil, garlic, and sugar into a screw-top jar and season with the salt and pepper. Screw on the lid and shake well.

3. Put the chicken in a bowl, add half the dressing, and toss well. Heat a ridged grill pan over medium–high heat until smoking hot. Add the chicken and cook for 8–10 minutes, or until golden and cooked through, turning once or twice.

4. Put the red onion, cherry tomatoes, and pomegranate seeds into a large, shallow bowl. Add the wheat berries, beets, and mint and toss. Divide the spinach among four plates, spoon the wheat-berry mixture over them, then arrange the chicken on top. Serve with the remaining dressing alongside for pouring over the salad.

Chicken & Couscous Salad

PREP: 25 minutes
COOK: 20 minutes
SERVES: 4

1 cup Israeli couscous

4 cooked beets in natural juices,
   drained and cut into cubes

1 small red onion, finely chopped

8 cherry tomatoes, halved

1 pomegranate, seeds only

juice of 2 lemons

2 tablespoons flaxseed oil

2 tablespoons olive oil

4 teaspoons tomato paste

pinch of sea salt

pinch of pepper

2 tablespoons coarsely chopped fresh mint

1 teaspoon black peppercorns, crushed

1 pound chicken breast strips

The beets in this salad turn everything a deep, vibrant red and glistens jewel-like with the pomegranate seeds.

1. Put the Israeli couscous into a saucepan and cover with boiling water. Bring back to a boil, then simmer for 6–8 minutes, or until just tender. Drain, then rinse and transfer to a shallow salad bowl. Add the beets, then the red onion, cherry tomatoes, and pomegranate seeds.

2. For the dressing, put the juice of one lemon, the flaxseed oil, half the olive oil, and half the tomato paste into a screw-top jar and season with the salt and pepper, screw on the lid, and shake well. Drizzle the dressing over the salad, then sprinkle with the mint and toss.

3. Put the remaining lemon juice, olive oil, and tomato paste and the crushed peppercorns into a clean plastic bag, twist, and shake well. Add the chicken, seal, then shake until it is evenly coated.

4. Heat a ridged grill pan over medium–high heat until smoking hot. Add the chicken and cook for 8–10 minutes, or until golden and cooked through, turning once or twice. Arrange the chicken over the salad and serve.

Bulgur wheat is a popular alternative to rice in many parts of the Middle East, particularly Syria and the Lebanon. This is a wonderful, filling vegetarian main dish, and it is perfect for a lunch box.

Bulgur Wheat Salad with Roasted Carrots, Mint & Almonds

PREP: 15 minutes
COOK: 40 minutes
SERVES: 4

13 carrots (about 1¾ pounds),
  cut into small wedges

2 teaspoons cumin seeds

2 teaspoons ground ginger

2 teaspoons sea salt flakes

¼ cup olive oil

1¾ cups bulgur wheat,
  rinsed and drained

⅔ cup blanched almonds, toasted

¾ cup coarsely chopped fresh mint

juice of 1 lemon

large pinch of pepper

1. Preheat the oven to 400°F. Mix together the carrots, cumin, ginger, salt, and 3 tablespoons of the oil in a roasting pan. Roast for 40 minutes, or until tender.

2. Meanwhile, put the bulgur wheat into a saucepan and cover with three to four times its volume of boiling water. Bring to a boil, then reduce the heat and simmer uncovered for 8–10 minutes, or until cooked but with some bite. Drain into a strainer, then pour in the remaining oil and mix. Let it steam dry in the strainer for a few minutes.

3. Transfer the bulgur wheat to the roasting pan with the cooked carrots. Add the almonds, mint, lemon juice, and pepper and mix well. Transfer to a bowl and serve hot or cold.

Cook's tip: To add extra vegetables to this dish, roast any of your favourite root vegetables with the carrots, or mix in chopped fresh baby spinach with the mint in step three. You could also add crumbled feta just before serving.

Light and summery, this couscous can be served with almost any Middle Eastern dish. It is the perfect accompaniment to grilled fish or fish tagines, because the herbs and lemon complement fish perfectly.

Summer Couscous with Herbs & Preserved Lemons

PREP: 15 minutes

COOK: 25 minutes

SERVES: 4

2 cups couscous

1¾ cups boiling water

½ teaspoon sea salt flakes

2 tablespoons olive oil

4 scallions, finely chopped
  or thinly sliced

⅓ cup finely chopped fresh flat-leaf parsley

⅓ cup finely chopped fresh mint

⅓ cup finely chopped fresh cilantro

1 tablespoon butter

½ preserved lemon, rinsed and
  finely chopped

1. Preheat the oven to 350°F. Put the couscous into an ovenproof bowl. Pour the boiling water into a heatproof bowl, stir in the salt, then pour it over the couscous, place a folded dish towel over the top, and set aside for 10 minutes, or until the couscous is tender and the liquid has been absorbed.

2. Drizzle the oil over the couscous. Using your fingers, rub it into the grains to break up the lumps. Toss in the scallions and half the herbs. Dot the surface with the butter and cover with aluminum foil or wet wax paper. Bake for 15 minutes.

3. Fluff up the couscous using a fork, then transfer it to a large salad bowl. Toss the remaining herbs into the couscous and sprinkle the preserved lemon over the top. Serve hot.

Cook's tip: *Fluffing up couscous is especially important, because it not only removes lumps but also aerates the grains.*

Broiling eggplants until blackened gives the dressing for this salad a wonderfully smoky flavor. Alternatively, they can be barbecued or roasted in a hot oven.

Red Cabbage & Baby Leaf Salad

PREP: 30 minutes
COOK: 20 minutes
SERVES: 4

2 carrots, shredded into ribbons using a swivel-blade vegetable peeler

350 g/12 oz red cabbage, shredded

⅓ cup raisins

4½ cups baby leaf greens (a mixture of red-stemmed and red-leafed lettuce and mache)

juice of 1 orange

pinch of pepper

Dressing

3 eggplants

3 garlic cloves, finely chopped

2 tablespoons tahini

3 tablespoons hemp oil

pinch of pepper

1. For the dressing, preheat the broiler to high and remove the grill rack. Prick both ends of each eggplant, using a fork, put them in the grill pan, and broil 2 inches away from the heat source for 15–20 minutes, or until blackened, turning several times. Let cool.

2. Arrange the carrots on a serving plate, top with the cabbage, then sprinkle with the raisins and baby greens. Drizzle with the orange juice and season with the pepper.

3. Cut the eggplants in half lengthwise and scoop the soft flesh away from the blackened skins and onto a cutting board, using a large spoon. Discard the skin. Finely chop the flesh, then put it into a bowl. Add the garlic, tahini, and hemp oil, season with the pepper, and mix. Spoon into a serving bowl and nestle in the center of the salad to serve.

Cook's tip: *When broiling eggplants, it is essential to cook them until they are black all over and the flesh is soft.*

Fennel is delicious with orange. This salad works well with Whole Spice-Crusted Red Snapper (page 70).

Quinoa Salad with Fennel & Orange

PREP: 20 minutes
COOK: 12 minutes
SERVES: 4

3¾ cups hot vegetable broth

1⅓ cups quinoa, rinsed

3 oranges

1 large bulb fennel, thinly sliced using a mandoline slicer, green feathery tops reserved and torn into small pieces

2 scallions, finely chopped

3 tablespoons coarsely chopped fresh flat-leaf parsley

Dressing
juice of ½ lemon

3 tablespoons extra virgin olive oil

pinch of pepper

1. Pour the broth into a saucepan and bring to a boil. Add the quinoa, then reduce the heat and simmer, uncovered, for 10–12 minutes, or until the germs separate from the seeds. Drain into a strainer, then transfer the quinoa to a salad bowl and let cool to room temperature.

2. Grate the zest from two of the oranges and put it into a screw-top jar. Cut any remaining peel and the pith away from all three oranges, using a small serrated knife, and discard. Hold each orange above a bowl and cut between the membranes to release the sections. Squeeze the juice from the membranes into the jar.

3. Add the orange sections, fennel slices, scallions, and parsley to the quinoa.

4. For the dressing, add the lemon juice and oil to the screw-top jar and season with the pepper. Screw on the lid and shake well.

5. Drizzle the dressing over the salad and toss. Garnish with the fennel tops and serve immediately.

Cook's tip: *It is much easier to thinly slice using a mandoline slicer, but a small, very sharp knife will also do the job.*

This light, fresh salad is perfect for late spring or summer lunches. Dill is popular throughout the Middle East, particularly in Iran and Turkey, where it is often paired with fava beans in a variety of dishes. If serving this salad on its own, it's great sprinkled with crumbled feta, or it's a wonderful accompaniment to Roasted Salmon with Spices, Pomegranate & Cilantro (page 84).

Freekeh, Fava Bean & Pea Salad with Dill & Pomegranate

PREP: 15 minutes
COOK: 50 minutes
SERVES: 4

1 cup whole-grain freekeh

2½ cups water

⅔ cup peas

⅔ cup shelled fava beans

3 scallions, thinly sliced

3 tablespoons finely chopped fresh dill

3 tablespoons finely chopped fresh mint

grated zest and juice of 1 unwaxed
    lemon, plus extra squeeze of juice

2 tablespoons extra virgin olive oil

pinch of sea salt

pinch of pepper

½ cup crumbled feta cheese (optional)

½ pomegranate, seeds only

1. Rinse the freekeh in several changes of cold water. Put it into a saucepan, cover with the water, and bring to a boil. Reduce the heat and simmer, covered, for 45–50 minutes, or until cooked but with some bite. Drain well.

2. Blanch the peas and fava beans in boiling water for 1 minute, then drain, refresh in cold water, and drain again. Add them to the freekeh.

3. Mix the scallions, dill, mint, and lemon zest into the salad. Stir in the oil and lemon juice and season with the salt and pepper, adding extra lemon juice, if you desire.

4. Serve the salad warm, sprinkled with the feta, if using, and pomegranate seeds.

Cook's tip: *Freekeh is young, green wheat that has been harvested early and then toasted and cracked. It has been cooked in the Middle East since ancient times.*

Sweet tomatoes, crisp salty pita chips, crunchy radish and cucumber, and a citrus dressing come together in this traditional Levantine salad. Use the best fresh tomatoes that you can find, such as heirloom varieties.

Fattoush

PREP: 15 minutes
COOK: 12 minutes
SERVES: 6–8

1½ pounds mixed tomatoes,
   coarsely chopped

¾ cup thinly sliced radishes

2 cups coarsely chopped cucumber

3 scallions, thinly sliced

3 large pinches of sea salt

pinch of pepper

2 tablespoons olive oil

3 large whole wheat pita breads,
   cut or torn into triangles

4½ cups mixed salad greens

Dressing

2 tablespoons extra virgin olive oil

juice of ½ lemon

1 teaspoon sumac spice

1. Mix together the tomatoes, radishes, cucumber, scallions, and a pinch of salt and pepper in a large, shallow salad bowl, using your hands.

2. Line a plate with paper towels. Heat the oil in a large, heavy skillet over medium heat. Working in batches, fry the pita breads for 4–6 minutes, or until crisp and golden, turning halfway through. Transfer to the prepared plate and sprinkle with the remaining salt. Repeat until you have fried all the pitas.

3. For the dressing, put all the ingredients into a screw-top jar, screw on the lid, and shake well.

4. Add the salad greens and pita chips to the salad bowl. Drizzle the dressing over the salad and toss. Serve immediately.

Cook's tip: *If you're preparing this salad in advance, keep the dressing, leaves, tomato mixture, and pita chips separate, and combine just before serving.*

This light salad makes an elegant appetizer, light lunch, or dinner. It also works well as a side dish for Lamb Kofte with Yogurt & Mint Dip (page 66), Whole Spice-Crusted Red Snapper (page 70), or Ras el Hanout, Garlic & Thyme Roasted Leg of Lamb (page 82).

Fig, Goat Cheese & Watercress Salad

PREP: 10 minutes
SERVES: 4

6 figs, halved lengthwise

¾ bunch of watercress

2¼ ounces soft goat cheese

⅓ cup blanched almonds, toasted

Dressing

2 tablespoons finely chopped fresh mint

juice of ½ lemon

1 tablespoon honey

1 tablespoon extra virgin olive oil

pinch of sea salt

pinch of pepper

1. For the dressing, whisk together the mint, lemon juice, honey, and oil in a small bowl and season with the salt and pepper.

2. Put the figs into a small bowl, drizzle with a tablespoon of the dressing, and mix gently.

3. Pile the watercress onto a large serving plate. Drizzle the dressing over the salad and toss. Sprinkle the figs, goat cheese, and almonds over the watercress. Serve immediately.

Cook's tip: *You can substitute other young salad greens, such as spinach, arugula, or baby Swiss chard, for the watercress in this salad, or use a mixture, if you prefer.*

Pickled vegetables are popular in the Middle East, and it takes just 30 minutes to lightly pickle your own beets. The soft goat cheese contrasts wonderfully with the crisp beets and sharp grapefruit.

Pickled Beet, Grapefruit & Goat Cheese Salad

PREP: 20 minutes
MARINATE: 30 minutes
SERVES: 4

8 raw beets, peeled and thinly sliced
    using a mandoline slicer

3 tablespoons white wine vinegar or
    apple cider vinegar

2 pinches of sea salt flakes

2 pink grapefruit, peeled and sectioned

4½ ounces soft goat cheese,
    cut into cubes

⅓ cup blanched almonds, toasted

¼ cup coarsely chopped fresh dill

Dressing

2 tablespoons extra virgin olive oil

2 tablespoons honey

2 tablespoons grapefruit juice

pinch of pepper

1 Mix the beets, vinegar, and a pinch of salt together in a large bowl. Cover and let marinate for 30 minutes.

2. For the dressing, whisk the oil, honey, and grapefruit juice together in a small bowl and season with a pinch of salt and pepper.

3. Pile the pickled beet, grapefruit, goat cheese, almonds, and dill onto a platter. Drizzle the dressing over the salad and toss. Serve immediately.

Cook's tip: *For an even more colorful dish, look for golden or bicolor beets when they are in season.*

This refreshing, crunchy summer salad has a wonderful balance of sweetness from the watermelon and saltiness from the feta, brought together beautifully by the lively mint dressing. Serve it as part of an outdoor summer salad spread on a hot day, pack it up for picnics, or enjoy it on a gloomy day to give instant indoor sunshine.

Summer Watermelon, Feta & Mint Salad

PREP: 15 minutes
SERVES: 4

2 cups cubed watermelon flesh
   (cut into ¾-inch cubes)

1 cucumber, cut into ¾-inch cubes

6 ounces feta cheese,
   cut into ¾-inch cubes

2 tablespoons fresh mint leaves

Dressing

¼ cup shredded fresh mint

juice of 1 lemon

2 tablespoons olive oil

pinch of sea salt

pinch of pepper

1. Mix the watermelon, cucumber, and feta together in a large bowl. Add the whole mint leaves.

2. For the dressing, whisk the shredded mint, lemon juice, and oil together in a small bowl and season with the salt and pepper.

3. Drizzle the dressing over the salad and toss, being careful the feta doesn't break up. Serve immediately.

Cook's tip: *If preparing this salad in advance, keep the watermelon, cucumber, and feta refrigerated in three separate containers. Make the dressing and store it in a fourth container. Combine all four elements just before serving to avoid the salad becoming watery.*

This crunchy salad puts pomegranate center stage instead of simply using it as a garnish. It makes a delicious and unusual part of a meze meal, but also works as an accompaniment to Chicken, Mushroom & Lemon Borekas (page 184) or Beef Sambousek (page 186).

Pomegranate Salad with Herbs & Pistachios

PREP: 10 minutes
SERVES: 4

2 large pomegranates, seeds only

1/3 cup finely chopped fresh cilantro

1/3 cup finely chopped fresh flat-leaf parsley

1/4 cup finely chopped fresh mint

1/4 cup unsalted pistachio nut halves

2 tablespoons extra virgin olive oil

juice of 1/2 lemon

1. Put the pomegranate seeds, cilantro, parsley, mint, and pistachio nuts into a large salad bowl and mix well.

2. Pour the oil over the salad and squeeze the lemon juice on top, then stir and serve.

Cook's tip: *You can prepare this salad in advance, then cover it and chill in the refrigerator. It is best eaten within a few hours of being made.*

This fresh, summery dish is delicious as part of a meze meal or served as an accompaniment to roasted chicken. "Smashing" the cucumber instead of slicing it gives the salad an unusual texture.

Cucumber, Radish & Sesame Salad with Lemon & Dill Dressing

PREP: 10 minutes
CHILL: 1 hour
SERVES: 4

1 cucumber, cut into 2-inch rounds

large pinch of sea salt

6 radishes, thinly sliced

5 teaspoons sesame seeds

Dressing

juice of 1 lemon

2 tablespoons pink peppercorns, crushed

¼ cup extra virgin olive oil

1 teaspoon tahini

2 tablespoons finely chopped fresh dill

large pinch of sea salt

1. Put the cucumber into a large freezer-proof bag and seal. Using a rolling pin, gently smash it into large, irregular chunks, then transfer them to a colander. Add a large pinch of salt and shake. Set over a bowl and transfer to the refrigerator for 1 hour, or until drained and firm.

2. Meanwhile, for the dressing, whisk all the ingredients together in a small bowl.

3. Mix the cucumber, radishes, and sesame seeds together in a salad bowl. Drizzle the dressing over the salad and toss. Serve immediately.

Cook's tip: *Cucumber salads often taste watery, but by salting the cucumber for an hour, you make sure it stays crisp and crunchy.*

Couscous combined with dried fruit and nuts is delicious served with grilled meats and spicy tagines. Traditionally, a fruity couscous would also be dusted with cinnamon and served on its own, often as a palate cleanser.

Spicy Couscous with Nuts, Dates & Apricots

PREP: 15 minutes
COOK: 10 minutes
SERVES: 4

2 cups couscous

1¾ cups boiling water

½ teaspoon sea salt flakes

2 tablespoons olive oil

¾ cup clarified butter

large pinch of saffron threads

⅔ cup blanched almonds

¾ cup unsalted pistachio nuts

1–2 teaspoons ras el hanout

¾ cup thinly sliced dates

¾ cup thinly sliced dried apricots

2 teaspoons ground cinnamon, to garnish

1. Put the couscous into a shallow heatproof bowl. Put the boiling water into a small heatproof bowl, stir in the salt, then pour it over the couscous, cover, and let stand for 10 minutes.

2. Drizzle the oil over the couscous. Using your fingers, rub it into the grains to break up the lumps.

3. Heat the butter in a heavy skillet over medium heat. Add the saffron, almonds, and pistachio nuts and cook for 1–2 minutes, or until the nuts begin to brown and emit a nutty aroma, stirring occasionally. Stir in the ras el hanout, toss in the dates and dried apricots, and cook, stirring, for 2 minutes. Fluff up the couscous, using a fork, then add it to the pan, mix well, and heat through. Remove from the heat.

4. Pile the couscous onto a serving plate in a mound. Rub the cinnamon through your fingers to create vertical lines from the top of the mound to the bottom, like the spokes of a wheel. Serve immediately.

Cook's tip: *Choose moist dates to ensure the salad is not dry.*

Dips, Preserves & Sauces

This popular Levantine eggplant dip is incredibly easy to make and is a perfect complement to freshly made pita breads (page 172). This is the Egyptian version, made with tahini and lemon juice. Other versions include slowly fried onions and tomatoes.

Baba Ghanouj

PREP: 15 minutes
COOK: 1 hour
SERVES: 4

1 extra-large eggplant

juice of 1 lemon

½ garlic clove, crushed

2 teaspoons tahini

large pinch of sea salt

2 tablespoons extra virgin olive oil

1 tablespoon coarsely chopped
  fresh flat-leaf parsley (optional)

8 pita breads, to serve (optional)

½ cucumber, cut into sticks,
  to serve (optional)

1. Preheat the broiler to medium–high and remove the grill rack. Prick the eggplant all over using a fork, put it into the grill pan, and broil 2 inches away from the heat source for 30 minutes on each side, or until soft and blackened all over and almost falling apart. Let cool.

2. Cut the eggplant in half lengthwise and scoop the soft flesh away from the blackened skin and into a bowl, using a large spoon. Discard the skin. Mash the flesh using a fork, then stir in the lemon juice, garlic, tahini, salt, and 1 tablespoon of oil.

3. Spoon the dip into a serving bowl, then drizzle with the remaining oil and sprinkle with the parsley, if using. Serve with pita breads and cucumber sticks, if using.

Cook's tip: *It's always a good idea to taste food just before serving and adjust the balance of flavorings, if you desire. You may want to add a little more lemon juice, sea salt, or garlic to this dip.*

Rose
Harissa
page 154

Homemade harissa is fresher and more vibrant than a store-bought version (if you can find it), and you can control the amount of chile, oil, and seasoning you include.

Rose Harissa

PREP: 15 minutes
COOK 3 minutes
SERVES: 10

2 teaspoons cumin seeds

1 teaspoon coriander seeds

1 teaspoon fennel seeds

8 red chiles, coarsely chopped

½ large red bell pepper, seeded and coarsely chopped

6 garlic cloves

¼ teaspoon rosewater

2 tablespoons olive oil

2 teaspoons sea salt flakes, plus a pinch

2 tablespoons dried rose petals

1. Heat a small skillet over low heat. Add the cumin, coriander, and fennel seeds and toast for 2–3 minutes, or until aromatic. Transfer to a mortar and pestle and crush to a powder.

2. Put the chiles, including the seeds, the red bell pepper, garlic, rosewater, oil, 2 teaspoons of salt, the spice powder, and half the rose petals into a blender and process until they form a paste with the consistency of homemade pesto; it should not be completely smooth. Stir in the remaining rose petals and season with a pinch of salt.

3. You can store the harissa, covered, in the refrigerator for three or four days.

› **Photograph on previous page**

Cook's tip: If you prefer a thicker harissa paste, reduce the amount of oil by half. If you prefer a more saucelike consistency, drizzle in more oil and adjust the seasoning accordingly. You can increase or decrease the number of chiles to taste.

This fresh, spiced yogurt dip is great served in little lettuce leaves as an appetizer or as a dip to go with vegetable sticks.

Spiced Beet & Cucumber Cacik

PREP: 20 minutes
SERVES: 4

2 cooked beets in natural juices,
  drained and cut into cubes
½ cucumber, cut into small cubes
⅓ cup small radish cubes
1 scallion, finely chopped
12 Boston, Bibb, or other small
  butterhead lettuce leaves

Dip

⅔ cup low-fat Greek-style plain yogurt
¼ teaspoon ground cumin
½ teaspoon honey
2 tablespoons finely chopped fresh mint
pinch of salt
pinch of pepper

1. For the dip, put the yogurt, cumin, and honey into a large bowl. Stir in the mint and season with the salt and pepper.

2. Add the beets, cucumber, radishes, and scallion, then toss.

3. Arrange the lettuce leaves on a plate. Spoon a little of the salad into each leaf. Serve immediately.

› **Photograph on following page**

Cook's tip: When spooning honey, heat the metal spoon so that the honey comes off more easily.

Spiced
Beet &
Cucumber
Cacik
page 155

This Syrian red bell pepper-and-walnut dip is popular throughout the Levant. It's somewhere between a thick hummus and an Italian pesto in texture. It's delicious scooped up with hot, crisp pita breads (page 172).

Muhammara

PREP: 25 minutes
COOK: 1 hour 10 minutes
SERVES: 6

3 red bell peppers

½ cup walnuts

⅔ cup fresh bread crumbs or
   ⅓ cup dried bread crumbs

1 tablespoon pomegranate molasses

1 teaspoon sea salt flakes

¼ cup extra virgin olive oil

juice of ½ lemon

pinch of crushed red pepper flakes

1. Preheat the broiler to medium–high and remove the grill rack. Line the grill pan with aluminum foil. Put the red bell peppers in the lined pan and broil 2 inches away from the heat source for 1 hour, or until blackened, turning occasionally.

2. Preheat the oven to 350°F. Transfer the hot bell peppers to a bowl, cover with plastic wrap, and set aside for 10 minutes to help steam off the skins.

3. Meanwhile, sprinkle the walnuts and bread crumbs on a baking sheet in a single layer and roast for 10 minutes, or until golden brown. Check them regularly, because they burn easily. Let cool to room temperature.

4. Peel the skins off the bell peppers and remove and discard the stems and seeds while retaining the juices. Put the bell peppers, walnuts, bread crumbs, pomegranate molasses, salt, oil, lemon juice, and crushed red pepper flakes into a food processor and process until smooth. Spoon into a bowl and serve as a dip.

Cook's tip: *We all have an individual preference for balance of saltiness, sweetness, acidity, and bitterness. Taste the Muhammara once blended, then adjust the consistency and taste with more olive oil, lemon juice, or salt, as required.*

Hummus with Garlic Toasts

PREP: 10 minutes
COOK: 3 minutes
SERVES: 4

1 (15-ounce) can chickpeas
  in water, drained with a little
  of the liquid reserved

juice of 1 large lemon

⅓ cup tahini

2 tablespoons olive oil

2 garlic cloves, crushed

pinch of sea salt

pinch of pepper

1 tablespoon finely chopped
  fresh cilantro

2 tablespoons Kalamata olives,
  pitted, to garnish

Ciabatta toasts

1 ciabatta loaf, sliced

2 garlic cloves, crushed

1 tablespoon chopped fresh cilantro

¼ cup olive oil

This makes a perfect quick-and-easy lunch served with pita breads (page 172) and is delicious as an accompaniment for a spread of Middle Eastern salads.

1. Put the chickpeas and a little of their reserved liquid in a food processor and process, gradually adding more of the reserved liquid and the lemon juice until you have the consistency you desire. Process well after each addition until smooth.

2. Stir in the tahini and all but 1 teaspoon of the oil. Add the garlic, season with the salt and pepper, and process again until smooth.

3. Spoon the hummus into a serving dish. Drizzle the remaining oil over the top and garnish with the cilantro and olives. Cover and chill in the refrigerator while preparing the ciabatta toasts.

4. Preheat the broiler to medium–high. Lay the ciabatta on the grill rack in a single layer. Mix the garlic, cilantro, and oil together and drizzle the flavored oil over the bread. Cook for 2–3 minutes, or until golden brown, turning once. Serve hot with the hummus.

Fava Bean & Mint Hummus

PREP: 20 minutes
COOK: 10 minutes
SERVES: 4

2⅓ cups shelled fava beans

2 tablespoons extra virgin olive oil

1 teaspoon cumin seeds, crushed

3 scallions, thinly sliced

2 garlic cloves, finely chopped

½ cup torn fresh mint leaves

⅓ cup finely chopped fresh
   flat-leaf parsley

juice of 1 lemon

¼ cup Greek-style plain yogurt

pinch of sea salt

pinch of pepper

To serve

1 red and 1 yellow bell pepper,
   seeded and cut into strips

4 celery stalks, cut into strips

½ cucumber, halved, seeded,
   and cut into strips

4 whole wheat pita breads

This summery hummus, made with freshly shelled fava beans flavored with chopped fresh herbs and lemon juice, is delicious on warm pita bread (page 172).

1. Fill the bottom of a steamer halfway with water, bring to a boil, then put the beans in the steamer top, cover with a lid, and steam for 10 minutes, or until tender.

2. Meanwhile, heat the oil in a skillet over medium heat. Add the cumin, scallions, and garlic and sauté for 2 minutes, or until the scallions are softened.

3. Put the beans in a food processor, add the scallion mixture, mint, parsley, lemon juice, yogurt, salt, and pepper. Process to a coarse puree, then spoon into a dish set on a large plate.

4. Arrange the vegetable strips around the hummus and serve with the pitas.

Cook's tip: *You will need to buy 1½–1¾ pounds fava beans in their pods and shell them.*

This piquant green Yemeni chili sauce goes well with boiled eggs, as a dip for Chicken, Mushroom & Lemon Borekas (page 184) or Beef Sambousek (page 186), or as a sauce to cut through the richness of roasted lamb. It takes only minutes to prepare in a food processor.

Zhoug

PREP: 15 minutes
SERVES: 6

1 cup coarsely chopped
  fresh cilantro

2 tablespoons coarsely chopped
  fresh flat-leaf parsley

1 preserved lemon, rinsed
  and coarsely chopped

1 garlic clove

6 green cardamom pods, seeds only

2 green chiles, seeded if you
  prefer a less spicy sauce,
  and coarsely chopped

½ teaspoon superfine sugar

½ teaspoon ground cumin

⅓ cup extra virgin olive oil

1 teaspoon sea salt flakes, plus a
  pinch to taste (optional)

1. Put all the ingredients into a food processor or blender and process until you have a smooth sauce. Season with a pinch of salt, if using.

2. You can keep the sauce, covered, in the refrigerator for up to three days.

Cook's tip: *If you do not have a food processor, very finely chop the cilantro, parsley, and preserved lemon and put them into a bowl. Crush the garlic, cardamom seeds, and green chiles together in a mortar and pestle and add them to the herbs. Stir in the sugar, cumin, extra virgin olive oil, salt, and 2 tablespoons of water and mix well.*

Labneh

PREP: 5 minutes
DRAIN: 4 hours
SERVES: 4

2 cups Greek-style plain yogurt

½ teaspoon sea salt flakes

Labneh is easy to make and is delicious drizzled with good-quality olive oil and sprinkled with sea salt and herbs as part of a meze meal. It's equally good served with desserts, such as Roasted Figs with Honey and Thyme (page 197), as an alternative to thick cream or ice cream. You will need a clean, damp piece of cheesecloth, a rubber band, and some string for this recipe.

1. Line a strainer with damp cheesecloth or a clean dish towel, then place it over a bowl. Mix the yogurt with the salt and put it into the prepared strainer. Bring the edges of the cloth up and gently twist them together to enclose the yogurt into a ball. You don't need to twist it tightly—just enough to hold the yogurt mix firmly. Secure the twist with a rubber band.

2. Let the yogurt drain for 4 hours; it should have the consistency of thick cream cheese. You can keep labneh in the refrigerator, covered, for up to two days.

Cook's tip: If you prefer labneh to have a firmer texture, let it hang overnight in the refrigerator. For quicker results, hang it on a cupboard door handle, using a piece of string, with a bowl set underneath it to catch the liquid.

Tahina Sauce

PREP: 10 minutes
SERVES: 6

1 teaspoon cumin seeds

3 garlic cloves

⅓ cup tahini

⅓ cup iced water

juice of 1 lemon, plus a squeeze to
    taste (optional)

2 teaspoons sea salt flakes, plus a pinch

pinch of pepper

As anyone who has tried to scrape the last spoonful from the jar knows, tahini (or ground sesame) paste is far too thick to use as a sauce. This popular Middle Eastern condiment blends it with lemon juice, garlic, and water to form a light sauce, which is perfect for slathering over wraps or into stuffed pita breads. Try it with Spicy Grilled Chicken Wraps (page 58) or as an accompaniment to Kibbeh (page 18).

1. Heat a small skillet over low heat. Add the cumin seeds and toast for 2–3 minutes, or until aromatic. Put into a mortar and pestle and crush to a powder.

2. Put the ground cumin, garlic, tahini, iced water, lemon juice, and 2 teaspoons of salt into a blender and process until smooth. You want the consistency of light cream. Season with a pinch of salt and pepper and add a squeeze of lemon juice, if using.

3. Keep the sauce, covered, in the refrigerator for two or three days.

Cook's tip: *The amount of garlic in the recipe gives the sauce a strong kick. If you prefer a milder garlic flavor, start with one clove, process, and add more, if you desire.*

It is worth having a stash of homemade preserved lemons in the refrigerator—they are really easy to make. You can use them to jazz up all kinds of dishes, from baked fish to roasted vegetables.

Preserved Lemons

PREP: 20 minutes
PRESERVE: 3 weeks
MAKES: 8 lemons

8 unwaxed lemons, washed and dried

½ cup sea salt flakes

1 tablespoon coriander seeds

1 bay leaf

1. Preheat the oven to 275°F. Wash a 1-quart jar in hot, soapy water, then rinse well. Place the jar on a baking sheet and put it into the oven to dry completely. If using a canning jar, remove and boil the rubber seal.

2. Using the palm of your hand, roll each lemon hard on the work surface to release its juices.

3. Using a sharp knife, cut a small disk from the stem end of each lemon, then stand the lemons upright. Cut a deep X shape through each lemon, stopping ½ inch from the bottom, then stuff each one with 1 tablespoon of salt.

4. Pack the lemons tightly into the jar, adding the coriander seeds and bay leaf as you work, and push them down well. If the lemons are small, add a few more following the method above to make sure they're squashed in before sealing the jar.

5. Set aside at room temperature. After three days, the jar should be full of liquid; if not, fill up with fresh lemon juice. Let steep at room temperature for three weeks. You can keep the preserved lemons in the refrigerator for up to six months.

Cook's tip: Once your preserved lemons are ready to eat, rinse them well in cold water before using them. You can thinly slice the peel and add it to dishes, or mash the pulp through a strainer and use the juice as a seasoning.

Throughout the Middle East, pickled vegetables are served with meze dishes. Turnips are traditional, but other pale vegetables, such as cabbage and cauliflower, can be given the same colorful treatment.

Pickled Turnips

PREP: 25 minutes
COOK: 5 minutes
PRESERVE: 2 weeks
MAKES: 1 (1½-pint) jar

4 turnips (about 1 pound), trimmed

1 small cooked beet in natural juices, drained and thinly sliced

1 fresh bay leaf

Pickling solution

1¼ cups water

⅔ cup white wine vinegar or apple cider vinegar

2 tablespoons sea salt flakes

4 garlic cloves, thinly sliced

1 teaspoon coriander seeds, crushed

½ teaspoon crushed red pepper flakes (optional)

1. Preheat the oven to 275°F. Wash a 1½-pint jar in hot, soapy water, then rinse well. Place the jar on a baking sheet and put it into the oven to dry completely. If using a canning jar, remove and boil the rubber seal.

2. To make the pickling solution, bring the water and vinegar to a boil in a nonreactive saucepan, then add the salt and stir until dissolved. Remove from the heat, stir in the garlic, coriander seeds, and crushed red pepper flakes, if using, and let cool.

3. Meanwhile, bring a saucepan of salted water to a boil. Add the turnips and simmer for 5 minutes, then drain and let cool. Peel them, then cut them into ¼-inch slices. Layer the beet and turnip slices in the prepared jar.

4. Strain the cooled pickling solution over the vegetables in the jar, making sure they are submerged; they must not be exposed to air. Tuck in the bay leaf, cover, and seal tightly.

5. Set aside in a cool, dark place for two days, turning the jar over once each day. Transfer to the refrigerator for 12 days before opening.

Cook's tip: *Pickled green chiles are popular in the Middle East. To make them, follow this recipe, but replace the turnips with 8 ounces green chiles. Halve the amount of the other ingredients and use a 12-ounce jar.*

Breads &
Pastries

Soft pita bread is made all over the Middle East and eastern Mediterranean. Freshly baked, often several times a day, it is served as an accompaniment to many meals. It is a simple, lightly salted dough and is traditionally baked directly on the bottom of a stone oven.

Pita Bread

PREP: 30 minutes
RISE: 2 hours 10 minutes
COOK: 10 minutes
MAKES: 6–8

1½ teaspoons active dry yeast

1¼ cups lukewarm water

3⅔ cups all-purpose flour,
   plus 4 teaspoons for dusting

1 tablespoon vegetable oil,
   plus 1 teaspoon for oiling

1½ teaspoons sugar

1 teaspoon sea salt flakes

1. Put the yeast and water into a large bowl and stir until dissolved. Add the flour, oil, and sugar, crush in the salt, and mix well.

2. Dust a work surface with 1 teaspoon of flour, turn the dough out onto it, and knead for 5–10 minutes, or until it is firm. Oil a bowl with ½ teaspoon of oil and put the dough in it. Cover with a damp dish towel and let rise in a warm place for 2 hours, or until doubled in size.

3. Preheat the oven to 475°F. Dust the work surface with 1 teaspoon of flour, turn the dough out onto it, and punch it down with the heel of your hand. Roll it up into a ¾-inch-thick roll, then cut it into six to eight ½-inch-wide slices. Roll the slices into balls, cover with a damp dish towel, and let rise for 10 minutes.

4. Line a baking sheet with parchment paper, then brush the paper with the remaining oil and dust it with 1 teaspoon of flour. Dust the work surface with the final teaspoon of flour and roll out the balls into 6–8-inch disks.

5. Arrange the disks, spread well apart, on the prepared baking sheet. Bake for 10 minutes, or until puffed up. Remove from the oven and cover with a damp dish towel to keep the bread soft.

Cook's tip: *To knead dough, fold it in half toward you, press it down, using the heel of your hand, lift, and rotate a little, then repeat and fold. Try not to add extra flour or oil to stop it from sticking to your fingers, because this will affect the texture.*

Turkish Flatbreads

PREP: 30 minutes
RISE: 1 hour 20 minutes
COOK: 40 minutes
MAKES: 8

6 cups all-purpose flour, plus
   4 teaspoons for dusting

1½ teaspoons fine sea salt

1 teaspoon ground cumin

½ teaspoon ground coriander

1 teaspoon sugar

1½ teaspoons active dry yeast

2 tablespoons olive oil, plus 1 tablespoon
   for oiling

1¾ cups lukewarm water

1. Sift the flour, salt, cumin, and coriander together into a large bowl and mix in the sugar and yeast. Make a well in the center, then stir in the oil and water. Bring everything together into a dough.

2. Dust a work surface with 1 teaspoon of flour, turn the dough out onto it, and knead for 5–10 minutes, or until it is smooth and elastic. Oil a bowl with ½ teaspoon of oil and put the dough in it. Cover with a damp dish towel and let rise in a warm place for 1 hour, or until smooth and elastic.

3. Dust the work surface with 1 teaspoon of flour, turn the dough out onto it, and punch it down with the heel of your hand. Knead for 1–2 minutes. Line a baking sheet with parchment paper, then brush the paper with ½ teaspoon of oil and dust it with 1 teaspoon of flour.

4. Divide the dough into eight pieces and roll them into balls. Dust the work surface with the final teaspoon of flour and roll out the balls into 8-inch disks. Cover with a damp dish towel and let rise for 20 minutes.

5. Heat a heavy skillet brushed with 1 teaspoon of oil over medium–high heat. Add a dough disk, cover, and cook for 2–3 minutes, or until lightly browned on the bottom. Turn over using a spatula, replace the cover, and cook for an additional 2 minutes, or until lightly browned on the second side. Keep warm while you cook the remaining dough disks in the same way, adding extra oil when you need it. Serve.

These enticing flatbreads, infused with roasted garlic, make a delicious addition to a meze meal. The citrusy sumac combines perfectly with the lemon thyme and salty feta, but you can improvise with your own favorite spice, soft cheese, and herb combination, if you desire.

Thyme, Feta & Sumac Flatbreads

PREP: 45 minutes
RISE: 1 hour
COOK: 20 minutes
MAKES: 4

6 garlic cloves, unpeeled

⅓ cup olive oil, plus ½ teaspoon for oiling

1 teaspoon sea salt flakes

1 cup lukewarm water

1 teaspoon honey

3 cups white bread flour,
  plus 1 tablespoon for dusting

1 teaspoon active dry yeast

2½ teaspoons sumac spice

2 teaspoons coarsely chopped fresh
  lemon thyme leaves, plus 8 sprigs

½ cup crumbled feta cheese

2 tablespoons extra virgin olive oil

1. Preheat the oven to 350°F. Coat the garlic with 1 tablespoon of the oil, put it into a small ovenproof dish, and roast for 10 minutes. Let cool a little, then press the cloves out of their skins into a bowl and mash with the salt. Add the water, honey, and the remaining oil and mix well. Turn off the oven.

2. Sift the flour, yeast, and 1 teaspoon of sumac into a large bowl and mix in the chopped lemon thyme. Make a well in the center, then stir in the garlic-and-water mixture. Bring everything together into a coarse dough.

3. Dust a work surface with 1 teaspoon of flour, turn the dough out onto it, and knead for 5–10 minutes. Oil a bowl with ½ teaspoon of oil and put the dough into it. Cover with a damp dish towel and let rise in a warm place for 45 minutes.

4. Divide the dough into four pieces and roll them into balls. Dust the work surface with 1 teaspoon of flour and roll out each ball into a 4–5-inch disk.

5. Dust a baking sheet with the final teaspoon of flour. Arrange the disks, spread well apart, on the tray. Top each with one-quarter of the feta, a sprinkle of sumac, and two sprigs of lemon thyme. Let rest for 15 minutes. Preheat the oven to 425°F.

6. Drizzle the breads with the extra virgin olive oil. Bake for 8–10 minutes, or until golden brown and crisp. Serve warm.

Pides

PREP: 25 minutes
RISE: 45 minutes
COOK: 1¼ hours
MAKES: 8

⅔ cup crumbled feta cheese

Dough

2¼ cups white bread flour,
   plus 2 teaspoons for dusting

1 teaspoon active dry yeast

1 teaspoon sugar

1 cup lukewarm water

2 tablespoons extra virgin olive oil,
   plus ½ teaspoon for oiling

1 teaspoon fine sea salt, plus a pinch

Roasted vegetable filling (optional)

1 red onion, cut into small chunks

1 eggplant, cut into small chunks

2 tablespoons olive oil

8 ounces cremini mushrooms,
   quartered or cut into eighths, if large

1 tablespoon ras el hanout

2 pinches of sea salt flakes

1 (14½-ounce) can diced tomatoes

¼ cup coarsely chopped fresh cilantro

2 tablespoons extra virgin olive oil

Spiced sumac meat filling (optional)

1 tablespoon olive oil

½ onion, finely chopped

2 garlic cloves, finely chopped

2 teaspoons sumac spice

1 teaspoon sea salt flakes

8 ounces fresh ground beef or lamb

1 (14½-ounce) can diced tomatoes

¼ cup coarsely chopped fresh cilantro

Pides, or boat-shaped Turkish pizzas, make a versatile and delicious light dinner or lunch. As with Italian pizzas, the choice of topping is only limited by your imagination. You need to prepare just one of these toppings to make eight pides. Alternatively, try roasted red peppers and goat cheese, or wilted spinach, garlic, and an egg.

1. For the dough, mix the flour, yeast, and sugar together in a large bowl. Make a well in the center and stir in the water, extra virgin olive oil, and 1 teaspoon of salt before bringing everything together into a sticky dough. Dust a work surface with 1 teaspoon of flour, turn the dough out onto it, and knead for 5–10 minutes, or until smooth and elastic. Oil a bowl with ½ teaspoon of oil and put the dough into it. Cover with a damp dish towel and let rise in a warm place for 45 minutes.

2. If you are making the vegetable filling, preheat your oven to 350°F. Toss together the red onion, eggplant, olive oil, mushrooms, ras el hanout, and a pinch of salt in a roasting pan. Roast for 30 minutes, then put into a large saucepan. Add the tomatoes, then swirl the pan around with ⅓ cup of water and pour into the pan. Bring to a boil, then simmer for 30 minutes. Stir in the cilantro, extra virgin olive oil, and a pinch of salt.

3. If you are making the meat filling, heat the oil in a skillet over medium–low heat. Add the onion and garlic and sauté for 10 minutes. Reduce the heat to low, then add the sumac and half the salt and cook for 1 minute. Increase the heat to medium, then add the meat and cook for 10 minutes, or until browned, breaking it up using a wooden spoon. Add the tomatoes, then swirl the pan around with ⅓ cup of water and pour into the pan. Bring to a boil, then simmer for 25 minutes. Stir in the cilantro and season with salt.

4. Preheat the oven to its highest setting. Preheat a pizza stone or baking sheet on a high shelf. Divide the dough into eight pieces and roll them into balls. Dust the work surface with 1 teaspoon of flour and roll out each ball into a long, flat oblong about ⅛ inch thick. Place 2 heaping teaspoons of a filling in the center of each oblong, then pull the long ends up so the filling is encased in a boat shape. Twist each end and sprinkle with the feta. Place the pides directly on the hot pizza stone and bake for 8–10 minutes, or until golden.

Cook's tip: *Put an ovenproof bowl filled with water in the bottom of the oven when baking. This creates steam and gives a good crust.*

These packages take their inspiration from Turkey, and they are best served hot.

Feta & Spinach Phyllo Packages

PREP: 25 minutes
COOK: 20 minutes
MAKES: 6

2 tablespoons olive oil, plus ½ teaspoon for oiling

8 scallions, coarsely chopped

2 (10-ounce) packages fresh spinach, coarsely chopped

1 egg, beaten

1 cup crumbled feta cheese

½ teaspoon freshly grated nutmeg

pinch of sea salt flakes

pinch of pepper

4 tablespoons butter

6 sheets of phyllo pastry

1 tablespoon sesame seeds

1. Preheat the oven to 400°F. Brush a baking sheet with the ½ teaspoon of oil.

2. Heat the oil in a wok or large skillet over medium heat. Add the scallions and sauté for 1–2 minutes. Add the spinach and sauté for 3–4 minutes. Drain off any liquid and let cool slightly.

3. Stir the egg, feta, nutmeg, salt, and pepper into the spinach mixture. Melt the butter in a small saucepan.

4. Brush three sheets of phyllo with some of the melted butter. Place another sheet on top of each one and brush with more melted butter. Cut each pair of sheets down the middle to make six long strips in total. Place a tablespoon of the spinach filling on the end of each strip.

5. Lift one corner of phyllo over the filling to the opposite side, then turn over the opposite way to enclose. Continue to fold over along the length of the strip to make a triangular package, finishing with the seam underneath.

6. Place the packages on the prepared baking sheet, brush with the remaining melted butter, and sprinkle with sesame seeds. Bake for 12–15 minutes, or until golden brown and crisp. Serve hot.

Cook's tip: *When working with phyllo, keep any unused pastry under a damp, clean dish towel until you are ready to use it, because it dries out quickly.*

Dates were a staple part of the nomadic Bedouin peoples'
diet, even in pre-Biblical times. The advanced civilizations
that followed replaced the date pit with an expensive
whole almond as a culinary joke. These little appetizers
go one step further, with the addition of feta and by
wrapping the dates in layers of buttered phyllo pastry.

Date, Almond & Feta Rolls

PREP: 20 minutes
COOK: 20 minutes
SERVES: 8

2 tablespoons butter

32 whole blanched almonds
   (Marcona, if available)

8 Medjool dates, halved and pitted

1 cup crumbled feta cheese

4 sheets of phyllo pastry

1. Preheat the oven to 350°F. Line a large baking sheet with
parchment paper. Melt the butter in a small saucepan.

2. Push two almonds into the flesh side of each date half. Lay the
dates on a work surface, skin side down. Place a small mound of
feta on each, then pat it down; you should have about the same
amount of feta as date.

3. Lay a sheet of phyllo on a work surface and cut it into strips a little
wider than the date halves. Place a date half at one end of each strip,
then roll the date up in the pastry. Using a pastry brush, brush the
end of the phyllo with some of the melted butter to stick the edge
down. Repeat until all the phyllo and dates have been used.

4. Place the packages on the prepared baking sheet and brush them
well with more melted butter. Bake for 20 minutes, or until crisp and
golden. Let cool slightly before serving—the date filling gets hot.

Cook's tip: *Medjool dates are known as the king of dates. They are
large and particularly soft and tend to be grown in the Middle East
and North Africa.*

Chicken, Mushroom & Lemon Borekas

PREP: 45 minutes
CHILL: 45 minutes
COOK: 25 minutes
MAKES: 32

Boreka dough

4⅔ cups all-purpose flour

2 teaspoons sea salt flakes, crushed

⅔ cup olive oil

¾ cup water

1 egg, lightly beaten, to glaze

Chicken filling

2 tablespoons olive oil

5 cups finely chopped cremini mushrooms

2 garlic cloves, finely chopped

12 ounces skinless, boneless
  chicken breasts, cut into ½-inch cubes

1 preserved lemon, rinsed and
  finely chopped

¼ cup finely chopped fresh
  flat-leaf parsley

juice of 1 lemon

2 tablespoons Greek-style plain yogurt

pinch of sea salt flakes

pinch of pepper

Cook's tip: *To freeze, put the filled, uncooked borekas between sheets of parchment paper, place them in a freeze-proof plastic container, seal with the lid, label, and freeze. Defrost them completely in the refrigerator before baking.*

These Middle Eastern pies combine crisp pastry with a lemony chicken-and-mushroom filling. Boreka pastry dough is tactile and easy to use, and once you've got the hang of rolling and crimping it, the possibilities for fillings are endless. These are good as an appetizer or for a light lunch or picnic snack.

1. For the dough, sift the flour into a large bowl and mix in the salt. Make a well in the center and stir in the oil and water, using a fork. Turn the dough out onto a work surface and knead for 20–30 seconds, then bring it together in a flattened disk (it contains a high proportion of oil, so you won't need to flour the surface). Wrap the dough in plastic wrap and chill in the refrigerator for 45 minutes.

2. For the chicken filling, heat the oil in a skillet over medium heat. Add the mushrooms and garlic and sauté for 5 minutes, or until softened. Add the chicken and preserved lemon and sauté for 2–3 minutes, stirring. Cover and cook for an additional 5 minutes, or until the chicken is cooked through.

3. Remove the pan from the heat and stir in the parsley and lemon juice. Let cool slightly, then stir in the yogurt, salt, and pepper. Break up any larger chunks of chicken, using a wooden spoon, then let cool.

4. Preheat the oven to 400°F. Line three large baking sheets with parchment paper. Divide the boreka dough in half, then divide these halves in half again, continuing until you have 32 pieces. Roll them into balls and cover them with plastic wrap.

5. On a clean, dry work surface, roll one ball into a 3-inch-diameter circle. Put 2 heaping teaspoons of filling on one side of the circle, then fold the pastry over into a semicircle shape. Holding the package in one hand, pinch and twist the edges together into an overlapping "rope" shape, working clockwise from one side to the other (alternatively, you can crimp the edges together using a fork). Transfer to the prepared baking sheets. Repeat with the remaining balls, keeping the unrolled ones covered with plastic wrap as you work.

6. Brush the packages lightly with the beaten egg. Bake for 20–25 minutes, or until golden brown and cooked through. The borekas are best served hot, but they can be served chilled.

Beef Sambousek

PREP: 35 minutes
CHILL: 45 minutes
COOK: 1 hour
MAKES: 32

Boreka dough

4⅔ cups all-purpose flour

2 teaspoons sea salt flakes, crushed

⅔ cup olive oil

¾ cup water

1 egg, lightly beaten, to glaze

Beef filling

⅓ cup pine nuts

2 tablespoons olive oil

1 teaspoon cumin seeds

1 large onion, finely chopped

2 garlic cloves, crushed

1 teaspoon ground ginger

1 teaspoon ground cinnamon

1 teaspoon ground coriander

1 pound fresh ground beef

¼ cup finely chopped fresh cilantro

½ cup Greek-style plain yogurt

pinch of sea salt

pinch of pepper

Cook's tip: *To freeze, put the filled, uncooked sambousek between sheets of parchment paper, place them in a freeze-proof plastic container, seal with the lid, label, and freeze. Defrost them completely in the refrigerator before baking.*

These spiced beef pies, popular in the Lebanon, make excellent snacks or party food. Use finely chopped cremini mushrooms instead of meat for a vegetarian version. You will need three to four baking sheets.

1. For the dough, sift the flour into a large bowl and mix in the salt. Make a well in the center and stir in the oil and water, using a fork. Turn the dough out onto a work surface and knead for 20–30 seconds, then bring it together in a flattened disk (it contains a high proportion of oil, so you won't need to flour the surface). Wrap the dough in plastic wrap and chill in the refrigerator for 45 minutes.

2. For the beef filling, toast the pine nuts in a skillet over medium heat for 2–3 minutes. Transfer to a plate and let cool.

3. Heat the oil in the skillet over low heat. Add the cumin seeds and cook for 1–2 minutes, or until aromatic. Add the onion, increase the heat to medium, and sauté for 10 minutes, or until golden brown, stirring occasionally.

4. Reduce the heat to low, add the garlic, ginger, cinnamon, and coriander, and cook for 2 minutes. Add the meat and cook for 5 minutes, breaking it up well using a wooden spoon. Increase the heat to medium–high and cook for an additional 10 minutes, or until well browned, stirring occasionally.

5. Remove the pan from the heat and stir in the toasted pine nuts and cilantro. Let cool slightly, then stir in the yogurt and salt and pepper to taste.

6. Preheat the oven to 400°F. Line three large baking sheets with parchment paper. Divide the boreka dough in half, then divide these halves in half again, continuing until you have 32 pieces. Roll these into balls and cover them with plastic wrap.

7. On a clean, dry work surface, roll one ball into a 3-inch-diameter circle (it contains a high proportion of oil, so you won't need to flour the surface). Put 2 heaping teaspoons of filling in the center of the circle, then carefully lift three edges of the pastry up toward the middle and pinch together to form a three-point star. Transfer to the prepared baking sheets. Repeat with the remaining dough balls, keeping the unrolled ones covered with plastic wrap as you work.

8. Brush the packages lightly with the beaten egg. Bake for 20–25 minutes, or until golden brown and hot through. These sambousek are best served hot, but they can be served chilled.

Chicken Bastilla

PREP: 40 minutes
COOK: 1 hour 10 minutes
SERVES: 4

3 tablespoons butter

4 sheets of phyllo pastry

2 pinches of sea salt

2 pinches of pepper

½ cup blanched almonds, toasted

1 tablespoon confectioners' sugar

½ teaspoon cinnamon

½ teaspoon orange flower water

Chicken filling

1 tablespoon olive oil

½ onion, finely chopped

pinch of saffron threads

1¼ cups boiling water

10½ ounces boneless chicken thighs,
   each cut into eight pieces

juice of ½ lemon

Egg filling

3 eggs, lightly beaten

1 tablespoon olive oil

Cook's tip: *If you're serving a crowd, double up the ingredients, using two sheets of phyllo between each layer. You will need a 9-inch dish and you may need to increase the cooking time.*

This traditional Moroccan festival pie combines sweet and savory ingredients, a classic Middle Eastern technique. The saffron, chicken, eggs, and sweet almonds come together in a delicate balance of flavors and textures. Traditionally, fine *warka* pastry is used, but phyllo works well. It's ideal for a picnic.

1. For the chicken filling, heat the oil in a medium saucepan over low heat. Add the onion and soften without browning for 10 minutes.

2. Grind the saffron in a mortar and pestle, then add the boiling water, swirl, and pour into a small bowl. Let steep. Add the chicken and saffron water to the onion and bring to a boil. Reduce the heat to low and simmer, covered, for 30 minutes, or until the chicken is cooked through.

3. Lift the chicken out of the cooking liquid into a dish using a slotted spoon. Increase the heat to medium–high and boil the liquid until reduced to 4–5 tablespoons of thickened sauce. Stir 2 tablespoons of the sauce into the chicken. Mix in the lemon juice and a pinch of salt and pepper. Cover and let cool.

4. For the egg filling, whisk the remaining chicken sauce into the eggs and season with a pinch of salt and pepper. Heat the oil in a saucepan over low heat. Pour in the eggs and cook, stirring, for 5–6 minutes, or until lightly scrambled. Transfer to a plate to cool.

5. Mix the almonds, sugar, cinnamon, and orange flower water together in a bowl. Put into a mortar and pestle and coarsely grind.

6. Preheat the oven to 400°F. To assemble the pie, melt the butter in a small saucepan. Brush a little of the butter around a 7-inch round cake pan, using a pastry brush. Lay a sheet of pastry over the bottom of the pan, brush with butter, then repeat with two more sheets of pastry in overlapping layers, letting it overhang the sides of the pan.

7. Spread half the egg filling over the phyllo, top with half the chicken filling, then repeat. Place the remaining phyllo on top and brush with butter. Spread the almond mixture over the top. Fold the edges of the top layer of pastry over the almonds, brush with butter, then fold each original overlapping layer of pastry back over the pie to form a concentric pattern, brushing with butter as you work. Finally, brush the whole pie with butter. Bake for 20 minutes, or until golden brown.

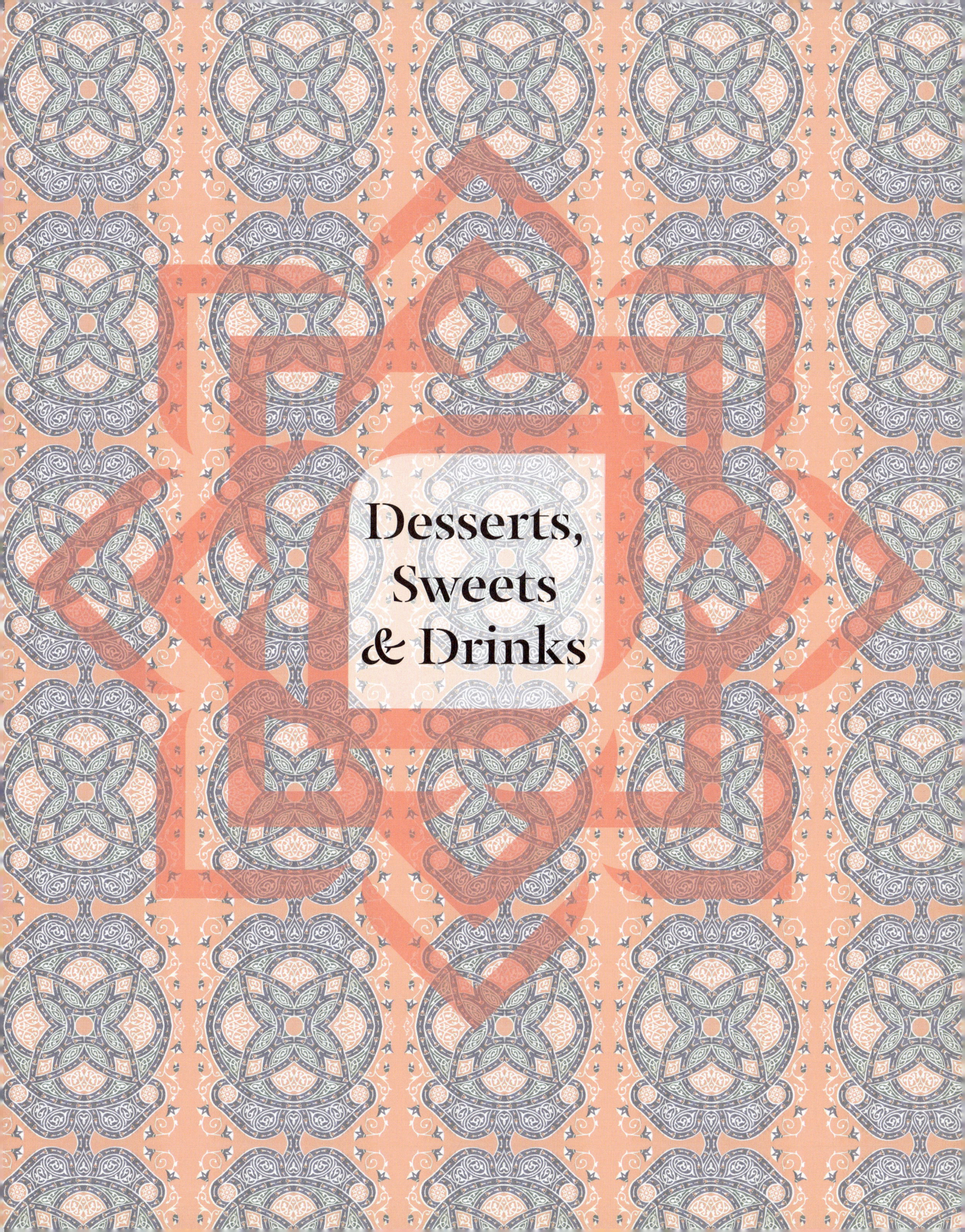
Desserts,
Sweets
& Drinks

This rich, scented rice pudding provides a comforting way to round off a Middle Eastern meal. The syrup adds a hint of sophisticated sweetness that enhances the creaminess of the rice.

Persian Rice Pudding with Rosewater & Cardamom Syrup

PREP: 10 minutes
COOK: 1 hour
SERVES: 4

11 green cardamom pods

½ cup basmati or other long-grain rice, rinsed well

3 cups milk

¼ teaspoon rosewater

⅓ cup superfine or granulated sugar

¼ cup water

1 teaspoon dried or fresh edible rose petals

1. Cut five of the cardamom pods in half, scrape the seeds into a mortar and pestle, and crush them. Put them into a saucepan.

2. Add the rice, 1¼ cups of the milk, the rosewater, and 2 teaspoons of the sugar to the pan and stir. Bring to a boil, then reduce the heat to low. Simmer for 1 hour, stirring occasionally and adding an extra ladleful of milk every 10 minutes, or when the rice has absorbed all the milk.

3. When the rice pudding is nearly ready, put the remaining sugar into a separate saucepan with the water, then cook over medium–low heat until the sugar has dissolved. Add the remaining cardamom pods and the rose petals, then simmer for 2–3 minutes, or until the syrup has thickened.

4. Serve the rice pudding hot, with the syrup drizzled over the top.

Cook's tip: *Cardamom pods come black and green. Black cardamom has a smoky flavor; green has a softer, more balanced flavor.*

Apricots
Poached in
Rosewater &
Cardamom with
Ginger Yogurt
page 196

This is one of the easiest desserts to make, and the apricots will bring some sunshine to the table. Your guests will be delighted by its exotic fragrance and gently spiced flavor.

Apricots Poached in Rosewater & Cardamom with Ginger Yogurt

PREP: 20 minutes
COOK: 15 minutes
SERVES: 4

¾ cup superfine or granulated sugar

6 green cardamom pods, lightly crushed

1 cinnamon stick

¼ teaspoon rosewater

1½ cups water

4 apricots, halved and pitted

1 tablespoon dried edible rose petals, to decorate (optional)

Ginger yogurt

½ cup Greek-style plain yogurt

1-inch piece of fresh ginger, peeled and finely grated

1. Put the sugar, cardamom, cinnamon, rosewater, and water into a saucepan, stir, and cook over low heat until the sugar has dissolved.

2. Increase the heat to medium–high, bring to a boil, then lower in the apricots, using a slotted spoon. Reduce the heat to low and simmer for 5 minutes. Turn off the heat and let them rest in the syrup for 10 minutes.

3. Transfer the apricots to a serving bowl, using the slotted spoon. When cool enough to handle, slip off and discard the skins.

4. For the ginger yogurt, put the yogurt into a small serving bowl, stir in the ginger, cover, and set aside.

5. Return the syrup to the heat and boil until reduced by half. Pour the syrup over the apricots, then sprinkle with the dried rose petals, if using. Serve the apricots with the ginger yogurt. If not serving immediately, let them cool, then cover and chill in the refrigerator and serve cold.

› **Photograph on previous page**

Cook's tip: Rosewater comes in different strengths, depending on the make. The one used for this recipe was strong, and the amount gives it a gentle rosiness. Adjust according to your brand and taste.

You don't need to do much with fresh figs, but roasting them is a wonderful way to bring out their flavor. This dish is perfect for a smart dinner party dessert, and no one will believe how easy it is to make. Use Greek-style plain yogurt instead of labneh if you are in a hurry.

Roasted Figs with Honey & Thyme

PREP: 10 minutes
COOK: 20 minutes
SERVES: 4

8 figs

10 sprigs of fresh thyme, broken
   into pieces

½ cup honey

½ cup labneh, to serve (optional)

1. Preheat the oven to 350°F. Using a sharp knife, cut a deep X shape through each fig, stopping just before it reaches the bottom, and stuff it with two pieces of thyme.

2. Line a small roasting pan with crumpled parchment paper, letting it come up the sides. Put the figs on the paper, drizzle a tablespoon of honey onto each fig, then sprinkle with the remaining thyme.

3. Roast the figs for 20 minutes. Serve two figs per person, hot, with the syrup in the parchment paper and a generous spoonful of labneh, if using.

› **Photograph on following page**

Cook's tip: *You can prepare this dessert in advance, then warm it through in the oven at 300°F for 10 minutes before serving.*

Roasted Figs
with Honey
& Thyme
page 197

People in the Middle East have for centuries packed dates as a provision for travelling through the desert. Here, with pistachio nuts and honey, they are delicious.

Date, Pistachio & Honey Slices

PREP: 30 minutes
COOK: 25 minutes
MAKES: 12

1¾ cups pitted and chopped dates

2 tablespoons lemon juice

2 tablespoons water

⅔ cup coarsely chopped pistachio nuts

2 tablespoons honey

Dough

1¾ cups all-purpose flour,
  plus 1 teaspoon for dusting

2 cups superfine or granulated sugar

1 stick plus 2 tablespoons (10 tablespoons)
  cold butter, coarsely chopped

¼–⅓ cup cold water

2 tablespoons milk, for glazing

1. Put the dates, lemon juice, and water into a saucepan and bring to a boil, stirring. Remove from the heat and stir in the pistachio nuts and 1 tablespoon of the honey. Cover and let cool. Preheat the oven to 400°F.

2. To make the dough, put the flour, sugar, and butter into a food processor and process to fine crumbs. Mix in just enough cold water to bind to a soft, not sticky, dough.

3. Lightly dust a work surface with flour. Divide the dough into two pieces, then roll out each piece to a 12 x 8-inch rectangle. Place a sheet of parchment paper on a baking sheet and top with a rectangle of dough. Spread the date mixture to within ½ inch of the edge of the dough, then top with the other rectangle of dough.

4. Firmly press the edges together, then trim the excess and score the top to mark out 12 slices. Brush with the milk to glaze. Bake for 20–25 minutes, or until golden. Drizzle with the remaining honey and turn out onto a wire rack to cool. Cut into 12 slices and serve.

Cook's tip: *Everything should be cold for making pastry, including your hands and work surface.*

The most evocative of Middle Eastern confectionery, Turkish Delight is headily fragrant, toothachingly sweet, and ever-so-slightly addictive.

Easy Turkish Delight

PREP: 20 minutes
COOK: 25 minutes
SET: overnight
SERVES: 6

4 gelatin sheets

1 cup water

1¼ cups granulated sugar

¼ teaspoon rosewater

a few drops of pink food coloring

1 tablespoon cornstarch

¼ cup confectioners' sugar

1. Line a shallow 7½-inch square dish or plastic container with heat-safe plastic wrap. Put the gelatin into a shallow bowl, just cover with cold water, and let soak for 5 minutes.

2. Squeeze the gelatin out well, then put it into a deep saucepan with the water and place over low heat until the gelatin has dissolved. Stir in the granulated sugar, rosewater, and food coloring, increase the heat to medium–high, and bring to a boil. Reduce the heat to low and simmer for 20 minutes without stirring. Boiling sugar is extremely hot, so handle with care and make sure it doesn't simmer over. Add more pink food coloring, if you desire.

3. Pour the mixture into the prepared dish and let cool to room temperature, then cover with more plastic wrap and chill in the refrigerator overnight.

4. The next day, mix the cornstarch and confectioners' sugar together on a large, flat plate. Place the Turkish Delight on the mixture and carefully peel away the plastic wrap. Cut it into squares, coating each one with the confectioners' sugar mixture as you work. Store in a sealed container and eat within a week.

Cook's tip: *Traditional Turkish Delight involves stirring the sugar for an hour or more, so this simple method is a real time saver.*

Wonderfully easy to make, these little clouds of lightly whipped cream look beautiful piled into your prettiest glasses. Your guests will love their Middle Eastern scent of cinnamon and orange flower water.

Cinnamon-Spiced Syllabub

PREP: 10 minutes
CHILL: 1 hour
SERVES: 8

juice of 2 lemons

½ teaspoon ground cinnamon,
   plus a pinch to decorate

1 teaspoon orange flower water

½ cup superfine sugar

2½ cups heavy cream

1 tablespoon chopped pistachios,
   to decorate

2 tablespoons pomegranate seeds,
   to decorate

1. Put the lemon juice, cinnamon, orange flower water, and sugar into a large bowl and whisk briefly to dissolve the sugar. Add the cream and lightly whisk until it just comes together as barely solid; this should take no more than 1 minute.

2. Spoon the syllabub into eight small, 4-ounce glasses. Sprinkle with the remaining cinnamon, the pistachios, and pomegranate seeds. Cover and chill in the refrigerator for at least 1 hour, or up to a day. Serve cold.

Cook's tip: *Syllabub should not be the texture of whipped cream, so be careful not to overwhisk it after adding the cream.*

Sometimes the simplest things are the best. The sticky tahini and date syrup perfectly complements the firm bananas.

Banana Flatbreads with Tahini & Date Syrup

PREP: 10 minutes
COOK: 5 minutes
SERVES: 4

4 (8-inch) whole wheat tortillas

4 tablespoons tahini

8 teaspoons date syrup

4 bananas, peeled

1. Preheat a skillet over medium–high heat. Add a tortilla and warm for 1 minute, turning halfway.

2. Arrange the tortilla on a cutting board, thinly spread it with a tablespoon of the tahini, then drizzle with 2 teaspoons of the date syrup. Add a banana, just a little off-center, then roll up tightly. Repeat with the remaining tortillas.

3. Cut each tortilla into thick slices, secure each slice with a toothpick, and arrange on a plate. Serve warm.

Cook's tip: *Store your tahini upside down when you first buy it; this will make stirring it much easier.*

These chunky, nutty bars use traditional Middle
Eastern ingredients in a modern way to create
a delicious raw snack.

Date & Coconut Bars

PREP: 30 minutes
CHILL: 3 hours
MAKES: 12

16 pitted Medjool dates, halved

½ cup unblanched almonds

½ cup cashew nut pieces

2 tablespoons plus 1 teaspoon chia seeds

2 teaspoons vanilla extract

¼ cup unsweetened dried coconut

½ cup coarsely chopped unblanched
   hazelnuts

¼ cup pecan halves

1. Put the dates, almonds, and cashew pieces into a food processor
and process until finely chopped.

2. Add the chia seeds and vanilla extract, and process until the
mixture binds together into a coarse ball.

3. Put a sheet of parchment paper onto a work surface and sprinkle
with half the coconut. Put the date ball on top, then press it into a
coarsely shaped rectangle. Cover with a second sheet of parchment
paper and roll out to a 12 x 8-inch rectangle. Lift off the top piece
of paper, sprinkle with the remaining coconut, the hazelnuts, and
pecan halves, then replace the paper and briefly roll out to press the
nuts into the date mixture.

4. Loosen the top paper and transfer the date mixture, still on the
bottom paper, to a tray. Chill for 3 hours, or overnight, until firm.

5. Remove the top paper, cut the date mixture into 12 pieces, and
peel off the bottom paper. Pack the date bars into a plastic container,
layering with pieces of parchment paper to keep them separate.
Store in the refrigerator for up to three days.

Cook's tip: *For a healthy addition to this snack, add 2 tablespoons
maca in step two. Maca is a root belonging to the radish family.*

Persian Love Cake

PREP: 45 minutes
COOK: 20 minutes
COOL: 1 hour
SERVES: 10

1 cup firmly packed light brown sugar

2 sticks (16 tablespoons) unsalted butter, softened, plus ½ teaspoon for greasing

4 eggs

1⅓ cups all-purpose flour

1¼ teaspoon baking powder

⅔ cup ground almonds (almond meal)

½ teaspoon ground cinnamon

6 green cardamom pods, seeds only

Rose mascarpone frosting

3¼ cups mascarpone

1¼ cups confectioners' sugar

¼ teaspoon rosewater

a few drops of pink food coloring (optional)

⅓ cup coarsely chopped pistachio nuts

1 tablespoon dried or fresh edible rose petals, to decorate (optional)

Love cake, according to legend, was made by a love-struck woman for a Persian prince, who promptly (and sensibly) fell in love with her upon eating it. There are numerous variations on Persian love cake, from dense, heavily spiced almond cakes, to fluffy angel food-style chiffon cakes, to lumpier nut-base yogurt cheesecakes. This delicate, carefully spiced layer cake, with a rose-scented mascarpone frosting, incorporates elements from all of these.

1. Preheat the oven to 350°F. Grease three 8-inch round springform cake pans with butter and line them with parchment paper.

2. Using an electric handheld mixer or wooden spoon, beat the light brown sugar and butter together in a large bowl until well mixed. Beat in the eggs, one at a time, beating well after each addition. If the mixture looks like it will split, sprinkle a little of the flour in with each egg.

3. In a separate bowl, mix together the flour, baking powder, almonds, and cinnamon. Crush the cardamom seeds in a mortar and pestle, then stir them into the flour mixture.

4. Fold the flour mixture into the egg-and-sugar mixture until incorporated. Divide the batter equally between the three prepared pans, level the tops, and bake for 20 minutes. To check the cakes are cooked, insert a toothpick into each one; it should come out clean. Let the cakes cool in their pans for 10 minutes, then transfer to a wire rack and let cool completely.

5. Once the cakes have cooled, make the frosting. Using an electric handheld mixer or wooden spoon, beat the mascarpone in a large bowl briefly until smooth. Whisk in the confectioners' sugar, rosewater, and enough food coloring, if using, to create a pale pink color. Spoon the frosting into a pastry bag fitted with a plain tip.

6. Pipe one-third of the frosting over one of the cakes in small minaret-shape mounds, then sprinkle with pistachios. Add another cake and pipe over half the remaining frosting in mounds, followed by more pistachios. Add the final cake, then pipe mounds over it in a design of your choice, before sprinkling with the remaining pistachios and the rose petals, if using.

Cook's tip: *The cake will keep for several hours at room temperature, but any leftovers should be refrigerated.*

Warm Walnut & Orange Cake

PREP: 45 minutes
COOK: 2¼ hours
SERVES: 10

3 large oranges (about 9 ounces each)

1 cup dried apricots

⅔ cup coarsely chopped walnuts, plus 12 halves to decorate

¾ cup coarsely chopped unblanched almonds, plus 6 whole to decorate

20 Brazil nuts, coarsely chopped, plus 12 whole to decorate

4 eggs

1 cup superfine or granulated sugar

½ cup light olive oil, plus ½ teaspoon for oiling

½ cup brown rice flour

2 teaspoons gluten-free baking powder

1 cup low-fat Greek-style plain yogurt, to serve

The classic orange cake is one of the most popular Middle Eastern treats. The cooked whole orange gives this one a tangy citrus hit. It's gluten-free, too.

1. Put one orange into a small saucepan, just cover with water, then bring to a boil, cover, and simmer for 45 minutes. Add the dried apricots, replace the lid, and cook for 15 minutes, or until the orange is tender when pierced with a knife. Drain the fruits, reserving the cooking water, and let cool.

2. Preheat the oven to 325°F. Lightly brush a 9½-inch round springform cake pan with oil. Put the chopped walnuts, almonds, and Brazil nuts into a food processor, then process until finely ground. Transfer to a large mixing bowl.

3. Coarsely chop the cooked orange and discard any seeds. Put the chopped orange and the apricots into the food processor and process to a coarse paste. Add the eggs, ¾ cup sugar, and the oil, and process until smooth.

4. Spoon the brown rice flour and baking powder into the ground nuts and mix well. Add to the food processor with the paste and process briefly, until smooth. Pour the cake batter into the prepared pan, spread it level using a spatula, and decorate with the walnut halves, whole almonds, and whole Brazil nuts.

5. Bake for 1–1¼ hours, or until browned, slightly cracked on top, and a toothpick inserted into the center comes out clean. Check after 40 minutes and loosely cover the top with aluminum foil if the nut decoration is browning too quickly.

6. Meanwhile, cut the peel and pith away from the remaining two oranges, using a small serrated knife. Cut between the membranes to release the sections. Measure ½ cup of the reserved orange cooking water, making it up with extra water, if necessary, and pour it into a small saucepan. Add the remaining sugar and cook over low heat until the sugar has dissolved. Increase the heat to high and boil for 3 minutes, or until you have a syrup. Add the orange sections and let cool.

7. Loosen the edge of the cake with a blunt knife and turn it out onto a wire rack. Let cool slightly, then cut into wedges and serve warm, with the oranges in syrup and Greek yogurt.

Baklava—a rich, sweet pastry made with phyllo, filled with nuts, and sweetened with either syrup or honey—is popular in Middle Eastern cuisine. This recipe is for the Turkish version and is made with honey and walnuts. It is popular on feast days.

Baklava

PREP: 45 minutes
COOK: 40 minutes
MAKES: 30

3½ cups finely chopped mixed nuts,
    such as walnuts, almonds, and/or
    pistachio nuts
1½ sticks (12 tablespoons) butter,
    plus ½ teaspoon for greasing
14 sheets of phyllo pastry
2 tablespoons sugar
1 teaspoon ground cinnamon

Syrup
1⅔ cups sugar
1¼ cups water
1 tablespoon lemon juice
3 tablespoons honey
2 small cinnamon sticks

1. Preheat the oven to 350°F. Line a baking sheet with parchment paper. Spread out the nuts on the prepared sheet and bake in the oven for 5–10 minutes. Do not turn off the oven.

2. Meanwhile, melt the butter in a small saucepan. Grease a 10 x 14-inch baking pan with some of the melted butter and place one sheet of phyllo on top. (Cover the unused sheets with a damp dish towel to prevent them from drying out.) Brush the phyllo with more melted butter. Continue layering the phyllo and brushing with melted butter until there are five layers of phyllo in the pan.

3. Mix the nuts with the sugar and ground cinnamon. Sprinkle one-third of the mixture over the phyllo, then cover with two more buttered layers of phyllo. Sprinkle half the remaining nut mixture over the phyllo and cover with two more layers of buttered phyllo. Sprinkle the remaining nut mixture over the pastry, cover with five layers of buttered phyllo, and fold in all the overhanging edges. Using a sharp knife, cut the baklava into diamond shapes, slicing through all the layers, then bake for 25–30 minutes, or until golden brown.

4. Meanwhile, make the syrup. Put the sugar and water into a saucepan, stir and place over low heat until the sugar has dissolved. Increase the heat to medium, bring to a boil, then add the lemon juice, honey, and cinnamon sticks. Reduce the heat to low and simmer for 10 minutes. Remove from the heat and let cool.

5. Pour the syrup over the baklava and let stand until the phyllo has absorbed all the syrup. The flavor of the baklava will mature for one or two days.

Sherbet, or *sharbat*, is a popular soft drink in the Middle East. It is a sweet syrup made from fresh flower petals or fruit, and here it is served as a long drink, diluted to taste with mineral or sparkling water. It can also be served over crushed ice and eaten with a spoon. This pomegranate-and-rosewater version is good with gin.

Pomegranate & Rose Sherbet Drink

PREP: 10 minutes
COOK: 6 minutes
SERVES: 8–10

juice of 2 lemons

¼ teaspoon rosewater

1 cup fresh pomegranate juice
   (juice of about 2 pomegranates)

1 cup sugar

crushed ice, to serve

8 fresh mint sprigs, to serve (optional)

mineral water or sparkling water, to serve

1. Put the lemon juice, rosewater, pomegranate juice, and sugar into a saucepan, stir, and cook over low heat until the sugar has dissolved.

2. Increase the heat to medium–high, bring to a boil, then reduce the heat to low and simmer for 3–4 minutes. Boiling sugar is extremely hot; handle with care and make sure it doesn't simmer over. Let cool completely.

3. Put some crushed ice into a tall glass. Pour a dash of the syrup over the ice and add a sprig of mint, if using. Pour in mineral or sparkling water to taste, mix well, and serve.

4. The syrup will keep in the refrigerator in a sealed container for three to four days.

Cook's tip: *To extract the juice from a pomegranate, cut it into eight sections, then squeeze each section into a strainer set over a bowl. Use the back of a spoon to extract the juice from any whole seeds that fall into the strainer. For a more floral sherbet, increase the amount of rosewater, drop by drop, tasting all the time; it can be overpowering if used too liberally.*

Mint Tea

PREP: 10 minutes
SERVES: 4

2 teaspoons Chinese gunpowder green tea

1 small bunch of fresh mint leaves

4 teaspoons sugar

This refreshing tea is Morocco's national drink, offered just about everywhere you go. It is also served at the end of a meal. It is prepared by brewing Chinese gunpowder green tea with fresh mint sprigs.

1. Warm a teapot by adding a little hot water, swirling it around, and then discarding the water. Put the tea into the pot, then add the mint, reserving four sprigs, and sugar.

2. Pour in enough boiling water to make four cups of tea and stir once, then let steep for 5 minutes. Pour into four tea glasses or cups and serve decorated with the reserved mint sprigs.

Apple & Tahini Juice

PREP: 10 minutes
SERVES: 1

2 apples, halved

1 small banana, peeled and coarsely chopped

2 tablespoons plain yogurt

1 tablespoon light tahini

½ teaspoon sesame seeds, to decorate

The banana and tahini gives this drink a distinctive Middle Eastern flavor. It's ideal for a midmorning pick-me-up or as a liquid breakfast.

1. Feed the apples through a juicer. Pour the juice into a blender, add the banana, yogurt, and tahini, and process until smooth. Pour into a glass, sprinkle with the sesame seeds, and serve.

Cook's tip: *If you don't have a juicer, you will need ½ cup fresh apple juice.*

For a sharp, refreshing drink on a hot summer's day, you can't do much better than a pitcher of fresh homemade lemonade. In this recipe the rosewater adds a wonderful floral twist.

Rose Lemonade

PREP: 15 minutes
COOK: 15 minutes
CHILL: 1 hour
SERVES: 4

finely grated zest of 2 unwaxed lemons

½ teaspoon rosewater

1¼ cups sugar

1 cup water

1½ cups lemon juice (juice of
   about 10 lemons)

2½ cups iced water

small pinch of sea salt

¼ cup fresh pomegranate juice

crushed ice, to taste

4 lemon slices, to serve

1. Put the lemon zest, rosewater, sugar, and water into a saucepan. Cook over medium–low heat, stirring continuously, until the sugar has dissolved. Let cool.

2. To make up the lemonade, pour 1¼ cups of the lemon juice into a pitcher, add three-quarters of the sugar syrup, 1¾ cups of the iced water, and the salt, and stir well. Taste, then add more iced water to dilute, more sugar syrup for sweetness, or more lemon juice for sharpness, according to taste.

3. To color the lemonade pink, stir in the pomegranate juice. Cover and chill in the refrigerator for at least 1 hour.

4. To serve the lemonade, divide the crushed ice among four glasses, then pour over the lemonade and add a slice of lemon.

Cook's tip: The lemonade will intensify in flavor as it chills, so you may want to dilute it a little more with iced water before serving from the refrigerator. If you accidentally overdilute it when making up the lemonade, and you can wait a few hours before serving it, just put it into the refrigerator until it has the right flavor balance.